BEE-ing Attraction

What Love Has To Do With Business and Marketing

A GUIDEBOOK FOR DEVELOPING A HEART-CENTERED BUSINESS & LIFE

Jan H. Stringer *and* Alan Hickman

Wyatt-MacKenzie Publishing
DEADWOOD, OREGON

BEE-ing Attraction
What Love Has To Do With Business and Marketing
A GUIDEBOOK FOR DEVELOPING A HEART-CENTERED BUSINESS & LIFE

by JAN H. STRINGER and ALAN HICKMAN

ALL RIGHTS RESERVED
©2009 by Jan H. Stringer and Alan Hickman
ISBN: 978-1-932279-32-0
Library of Congress Control Number: 2009926786

No part of this publication may be translated, reproduced, or transmitted in any form or by any means, in whole or in part, electronic or mechanical, including photocopying, recording, or by any information storage or retrieval system without prior permission in writing from the publisher.

Author Photographs © 2009 Daniel Quat

Publisher and editor are not liable for any typographical errors, content mistakes, inaccuracies, or omissions related to the information in this book.

Product trade names or trademarks mentioned throughout this publication remain property of their respective owners.

Please note, some individuals who have contributed to this book have chosen to use only their first name.

PerfectCustomers, Inc.
4711 Contenta Ridge, Santa Fe, NM 87507
jan@perfectcustomers.com, alan@perfectcustomers.com
(505) 474-5348

Wyatt-MacKenzie Publishing, Inc.
DEADWOOD, OREGON

www.WyMacPublishing.com
(541) 964-3314

Requests for permission or further information should be addressed to:
Wyatt-MacKenzie Publishing, 15115 Highway 36,
Deadwood, Oregon 97430

DEDICATION

*We dedicate this book to Slade and Sloan,
our grandsons, and, all children,
young and old,
who are committed to play, imagination, and creativity.*

ACKNOWLEDGMENTS

We would like to thank the many people who were supportive and instrumental in this book becoming a published reality. This includes our families, friends, and customers who have been so encouraging to us along the way. We thank all of our perfect customers, SACAT Coaches, Mentors, and Teachers for teaching us what we needed to know, and stuck with us during our learning curves. Additionally we thank the wonderful connection to the Energy where all is possible and which is the life force running through us as we took the actions to complete this goal. Thank you to our publisher, who held a long-standing vision for publishing our book, kept us focused and moving ahead.

JAN H. STRINGER *and* ALAN HICKMAN

TABLE OF CONTENTS

INTRODUCTION 1

PART I
Guidelines for Developing a Heart-Centered Business

CHAPTER 1: Develop a Heart-Centered Business 7
   Kitchen Table Planning: Birth of the SACAT Program
   — PATTY WALTERS 13

CHAPTER 2: Speaking and Sharing from the Heart 17
   My Defining Moment — PATTY WALTERS 26

CHAPTER 3: What Makes You Tick? 29
   Holding Myself Back…Nevermore! — SUZY GIRAUD 33
   Branding from the Heart: How a Strange Little Question
   Transformed My Business and My Life — JULIA D. STEGE 35

CHAPTER 4: Creating Your BEE-ing 39
   The Day I Stepped into the BEE-ing of CEO — DOUG UPCHURCH .. 50

CHAPTER 5: Why Are You Attracting What You Are Attracting…Again? 55
   The Divine Miss Em — EMILY DABNEY 63

CHAPTER 6: Trust, Intuition, and Inner Guidance 67

CHAPTER 7: Signs Guide the Way 79
   What Are Your Road Signs? — BETTY HEALEY 89

CHAPTER 8: Energy Balance and Attraction 91
   Good Vibrations: Staying Balanced through the
     Storm — JULIA D. STEGE 100

CHAPTER 9: You Are Always in the Perfect Place at the Perfect Time ... 105
   When the Timing Was Perfect for Me — MARIAEMMA PELULLO-WILLIS ... 111

CHAPTER 10: The Art of Mastering Space 115
   Stuck in Mexico — WENDY E. 130

CHAPTER 11: Planting Seeds of Intention for the Future 133
   Tiara: The Exceptional Woman's Coaching Program — BETSY SOBIECH 139

PART II
Creating Your BEE-ing Attraction Plan and Taking Action

CHAPTER 12: The BEE-ing Attraction Plan Is About a Deeper Connection 145
    Connecting with Who I Really Am — ANNIE SHERWOOD 150

CHAPTER 13: What Is Perfect for You? 153
    Attracting My Knight in Shining Armor — JENNIFER TANGUY 155

CHAPTER 14: Creating a BEE-ing Attraction Plan 157
    A Spark That Lights Fires — WENDY WATKINS 178
    Skeptical Me — Out to Prove You Wrong! — SUSIE DUKE 180

CHAPTER 15: Setting Goals in the Energy of BEE-ing 183
    To Have What You Don't Have, You Get To BEE Who
    You Aren't BEE-ing — ALAN DAVIDSON. 193

RESOURCES 199

ABOUT THE AUTHORS 205

INDEX 207

INTRODUCTION

STRATEGIC ATTRACTION™ Planning was first introduced by our company as a marketing technique which focused on building key relationships in business. Our method has been highly effective in helping business owners clarify and define what they would call a "perfect fit" for their core values. The strategy is described as a one-size-fits-all method because it can be applied to any type of relationship, is applicable to every kind of business, and adapts to all markets. The global best-selling book *Attracting Perfect Customers. The Power of Strategic Synchronicity*, which Jan Stringer co-authored, released the Strategic Attraction™ planning process to the world.

As we now release this second book, we are building on a journey of evolution and success! It is a joy to share what has become clear to us, and how it's all about LOVE. We thank the many loyal readers and subscribers who contributed to the growth of our training and understanding. We immensely appreciate our customers who were generous enough to share their personal stories and benefits they have experienced as a result of applying these concepts of Strategic Attraction™ in their

> *The plan is a tool for gaining deeper understanding of the inner workings of a business that contribute to personal fulfillment and success.*

businesses. It is an honor to have this opportunity to share with you what has worked for thousands of people to create and attract what they love in their business and personal relationships. We feel the most important things we could show are the successes that our perfect customers have received. You—the loyal readers, subscribers, clients, and customers—have been the greatest teachers and each of you has helped to bring this new book forward. It was your questions and real-life situations that we learned from, and now we delight in sharing what we have learned.

As our customers evolve and change, so has our understanding of our own process. We saw that the Strategic Attraction™ Plan was not just another four-step process; it had become a tool for gaining deeper understanding of the inner workings of a business that contribute to personal fulfillment and success. The people who have benefited from using this process in their business, along with the Licensed and Certified Strategic Attraction™ Coaches of SACAT (Strategic Attraction™ Coaches Academy and Training), know that it is about connecting to their soul and aligning their *BEE-ing* to their purpose.

Thus, we renamed the process the "BEE-ing Attraction Plan" to emphasize the aspect of being, or *BEE-ing,* which is the intended outcome of an attraction plan! To simplify the complex subject of being, we added an element of play by altering the spelling to make it more fun. In our world, being, or "BEE-ing" is what a bumblebee does—even though their bodies are not aerodynamically designed to to fly, they do it anyway. That's what our method is all about—learning to adopt the BEE-ing that will attract what others may say is impossible.

When you delve into each of the chapters and the stories that follow, and begin to apply the BEE-ing Attraction concepts into your business, you may notice that many parts of your life will begin to rapidly shift. Truth always causes an alignment inward, and at

JAN H. STRINGER *and* ALAN HICKMAN

the same time you will outwardly shift your business and the relationships around you. When what is most important to you aligns itself with your higher purpose in life, your BEE-ing causes a vibration that sends out waves of energy. The overall goal is to create a business, and a life, that you love because it feels good to you and to those around you.

Each chapter describes different concepts that you can apply to develop your heart-centered business. The guidelines included in Part I are consciousness-building or for personal expansion. Part II contains the steps to create your BEE-ing Attraction Plan. If you read the first book, we invite you to play along with this revamped and energized new model of the Strategic Attraction™ plan. If you are completely new to the process, open your mind and enjoy the ride!

You will learn to become more creative and imaginative as you design a plan for what you want others to expect of you rather than attempting to live life by what you think others might want from you. BEE-ing Attraction is about understanding that you have the ability to transform and heal all situations by first stepping into the BEE-ing of what is most perfect for you.

It helps you to fine-tune your energy to be a match for what you truly desire to attract. It gives you the encouragement to make the changes that you need to make and to have the healing you require. It eliminates sacrificing, shortens suffering, and it makes you the author of your life; 100 percent responsibility lies in your own hands. Finally, the BEE-ing Attraction process is about living attuned with what makes you tick, while sharing your unique talents and gifts with others. It is the beginning of doing something that is in alignment with what is most important to you. In essence, living true to your inner BEE-ing is like turning on your power switch and sending your light to a broader reach of people. Your inner light will shine more brightly as a result. Now that's attractive!

BEE-ing Attraction has already begun! How do we know?

We know that when you activated your power to attract, this book found its way into your hands. Perhaps your connection to our message happened in a way that may have seemed serendipitous or involved a synchronicity. More than likely, your intuition picked up the signal that now was the time. The how or why doesn't matter—the important point is that you are reading this right now!

Enjoy the process that will allow you to have more clarity and focus, and accelerates your ability to attract a business that supports you in having success and fulfillment as soon as possible.

From Our Hearts to Yours,
Jan H. Stringer & Alan Hickman

*Guidelines for Developing a
Heart-Centered Business*

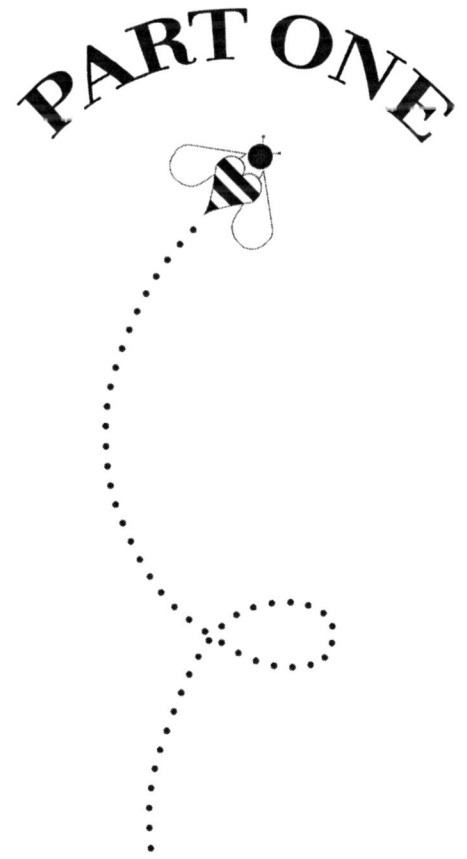

Chapter ONE

Develop a Heart-Centered Business

"People have important things to communicate. Speaking from your heart allows the emotionally difficult, the ordinary, and the wonderful things in our lives to be communicated and received."

—DAVID MᶜARTHUR AND BRUCE MᶜARTHUR, *THE INTELLIGENT HEART*

WISDOM comes in the most interesting ways—like when a child points out something so obvious, yet filled with simple truth. In this case, the simple truth came from one of our customers with whom we had the good fortune to share in a realization about what matters is BEE-ing a heart-centered business.

Marty was filled with emotion at the end of the training as he confessed that he hadn't wanted to attend this business retreat in the first place. He said he had only come because one of his friends had encouraged him to go. Marty told his friend he would attend with the caveat, "if they ask me to take my shoes off, I am leaving." He wasn't comfortable about what the retreat might entail. Now at the closing ceremony of the retreat, four days after his arrival, he recounted the story with the whole group while laughing and crying at the same time. He shared that his life changed forever out of the experience of BEE-ing at the retreat. Marty shared that he was so glad that he had not left on that first day even though he was asked to remove his shoes before entering the training room.

After returning home, his partner asked him what the retreat was all about. Marty responded, "Love." His partner looked bewildered by his answer and said, "What does LOVE have to do with business and marketing?" Marty looked back at his partner and replied, "Everything!" Marty's answer summed up that love is everything when it comes to business—it is at the heart of marketing and building a business; it's a simple truth.

This chapter is a basic introduction to our concept of building a heart-centered business. If you are just learning about our planning process for the first time, you will be learning how to attract business relationships that you would call a "perfect fit" for your business, as well as gaining a deeper understanding of how to develop a heart-centered business. The BEE-ing Attraction Planning process is the initial step in any marketing process. Many people use the process to help brand their products and identify what makes them tick, so that their markets are in alignment with what that they want to pursue in their business. The planning process is a way of building relationships and can help you to gain marketing insights into what is perfect for your heartfelt business.

"Writing a BEE-ing Attraction Plan has inspired me in two ways. First, describing my perfect customer brought me clarity about whom I want to attract into my business. Secondly, getting my goals on paper ignited the passion within and has focused me on critical 'attractive' actions. I am grounded, focused; attracting my perfect customers and all that I have asked for is magically appearing." —STELLA H.

When people are asked about their definition of marketing, they usually share that it is about getting the word out or other traditional methods such as advertising or promotion. In the past few years of working with business owners, the common language that each person spoke was that they wanted to do something that they loved for a living. When business owners love what they are doing for a living, you know it. You receive the warmth of their enthusiasm, the attractiveness of their passion, and the glow of their desire to share their gifts of understanding. As a consumer, we want to do business with people who love what they do, because it feels good to us to be in the presence of someone who is doing what they love.

If you are reading this and have studied in traditional schools, no doubt there were no courses offered about following your heart in business. More than likely, at one time or another, you may have felt or been trained that hard work was the only way to earn a living, and whether you enjoyed your job or profession was less important than the satisfaction of loving the work.

It is our belief that people are attracted to heart-centered businesses that radiate love and heartfelt feelings to their customers through their service, products, and programs more than their hard work ethic. When you are the customer or client of a heart-centered business, you know that the owner(s) are directly connected to their own heart and their passion. The contrast is also true—it becomes apparent when you are working with someone who is not heart-centered. Their business expression comes through as hype, pressure, easy money, too good to be true—which brings up uncomfortable feelings of being taken advantage or being ripped off.

The time is now to create a business that connects your heart and soul to your goals.

Now the times have changed and it signals new opportunities to be creative. Perhaps you might recognize this as a time to seek personal freedom and creative license to apply your heartfelt unique skills, and talents in a business of your own.

Hopefully you are ready to stop attempting to conform to the old business models, which were centered on chasing money in a dog-eat-dog world. Maybe you have been laid off from your job, been given "early retirement," or you are one of the many people caught in a company downsizing forced to consider new alternatives to earn a living. Whatever the reason you consider starting a business, this is a great opportunity to develop a heart-centered business—the timing is perfect!

A steady change has started to occur in the United States and the world, the results of which have yet to be seen at the time of this writing. You and everyone else are feeling the shifts that are causing one to embrace the massive changes taking place, and as uncomfortable as these times may be, change brings innovation and birth. In the face of changed economic outcomes, the fall of systems, the failures in the various industries, and the unpredictable effects of the stock market, you can rise above it all as effective and successful business owners. When you are the owner of a business that you love, you can succeed in any economy. The time is now to create a business that connects your heart and soul to your goals.

The guidelines recommended in the chapters that follow will help you to have an inner connection to your business and your goals. Additionally, these suggestions will become more enhanced and successful when you also supplement your business growth with personal healing and energy clearing to release past patterns to make room for a new beginning. (See Chapter 8).

What you have learned in your previous experience about the way business is done may need to be forgotten! To become successful, it may be necessary to let go of knowledge that you may have spent years mastering.

> *"I want it, but to have it, I must release it.*
> *And in the releasing of it, it comes easily."*
> —ABRAHAM-HICKS, SAN FRANCISCO 8/9/08

JAN H. STRINGER *and* ALAN HICKMAN

If your business was created to be a moneymaking machine at the expense of health and relationships, you may now desire to establish more lasting relationship connections with your business clientele and associates. Things that were effective before may not be producing the same results; therefore, change is necessary. It's time to implement a new way for your business to flourish and that starts with developing what is in your heart.

It takes courage to express what you truly want from a deep connection and believe that you can have anything that you truly desire.

Using the BEE-ing Attraction Planning process, which is explained in detail in Part II, will give you a new perspective and immediate practices to apply to your business during any economy. Use this book as your focus to develop a heart-centered business and enjoy the changes that are upon you, and forget what the news reports are saying!

> *"Focus on what is in your heart and stay centered on what is or you will create what isn't into what is!"* —ZOE

If you are someone who is developing a heart-centered business, here are a few qualities, characteristics, and attributes that might be present in your BEE-ing Attraction Plan:

- BEE-ing present in the moment
- follows their intuition; trusts their gut
- uses imagination
- expresses creativity through business
- courageous enough to stand for loving our self and each other
- radiates inner peace
- steps out in faith
- trusts their own process

- their business, relationships, and communities are centered around love and harmony
- walks their talk every moment
- hangs out with other like-minded people who bring the best out in others
- makes choices from their heart
- stands by their friends, partners, and associates

As you design and work with the BEE-ing Attraction Plan (see Part II of the book), you may notice that some of the previous ways that you have operated in business will not be in alignment with your heartfelt values. It takes courage to express what you truly want from a deep connection, and to believe that you can have anything that you truly desire. You can attract anything that you are willing to declare that you want to have in life, and the BEE-ing Attraction Plan is a springboard from which to gain clarity about what is perfect for you. Most of the people that have experienced the benefits of working with their BEE-ing Attraction Plan say that it was the permission they needed to create from a heart place rather than from what they thought was expected of them. It was also a way to connect with their heart and soul, and to make this a priority in building their business and in forming their relationships.

Use this book to guide your heart-centered business to:
1. gain **clarity** about the relationships you want to attract, as well as, what is a perfect fit for you and your business;
2. gain **focus** about what is the perfect next action to take to forward your business;
3. develop a **deeper understanding** about yourself so that your business is a true match for what is most important to you in life, and therefore is a business that is in alignment with your heart and soul.

JAN H. STRINGER *and* ALAN HICKMAN

After working with our book and planning process, you will never perceive your business, any relationship, or situation in quite the same way. We believe that business is very personal and it is a great place for you to express what is most important to you. Or as we say, "what is most perfect for me"! This is an opportunity to use your imagination and creativity to design a business that is worthy of your devotion.

"I really like the process we were taught. It seems to me, it is really about self-knowledge. It only takes place on the inside. It does not take place inside someone else or someplace else. We create our world by self-contemplation. What we contemplate ourselves to be, we are. My understanding is that the Universal Intelligence (God or whatever you want to call it) is characterized by three distinct attributes: it fills all space, it is amenable to suggestion, and it works only by deductions. By deduction I mean that it takes its creative direction from the word you give it. It does not decide nor initiate. It only responds with creative force. It does not operate any other way. It becomes for you whatever you want it to be."
—FROM A STUDENT OF SACAT COACH EVA GREGORY

CUSTOMER STORY

Kitchen Table Planning: Birth of the SACAT Program
BY PATTY WALTERS, MASTER STRATEGIC ATTRACTION™ COACH

"Men start their businesses in the garage; Women start theirs around the kitchen table!"—JAN H. STRINGER

My first experience of using a "Kitchen Table Planning Process" was working with Jan Stringer, founder of PerfectCustomers, Inc. around her kitchen table in her home in Houston, Texas, also known as *world headquarters*.

JAN H. STRINGER *and* ALAN HICKMAN

I was always amazed when Jan would pull out the planning boards to show me the projects she was either thinking about or the ones that were in motion. I loved the look of them—bright white boards with wonderful colors of sticky notes, with coordinating colored markers used to write the words. I've always been fascinated by color and writing words down in various ways.

Let me back up a bit and tell you about the actual location that was world headquarters for Perfect Customers, Inc. The house was built about 1920 and was located in a historical area of Houston called "The Heights." The Heights has some magical properties to it and actually feels like a small town within a big city. The big city, if you will, is a mere stone's throw from this place that seems to be caught somewhere in time. Old homes lovingly renovated, new homes built to look old and buildings in disrepair are all mixed together among beautiful trees, magnificent flowers, and greenery.

Headquarters resided in a yellow two bedroom renovated bungalow (Jan and Alan called it the "Golden House" or "Gold-In-House") on a beautiful tree-shaded lot. It had warm wood floors, a small, cozy kitchen, and many windows to access all of the beautiful trees and plants growing on the property. This was butterfly and hummingbird heaven. The front of the house had a wonderful porch that reached across the entire front. On the porch were many beautiful plants, which Alan lovingly tended to, a wonderful laughing fountain, and of course, a porch swing. Coming up to the front porch was a small walkway and hanging over the top step as you entered the porch area hung some wonderful art pieces from tiny hooks. They were actual words that hung vertically and they delighted my soul every time I saw them. One said "Harmony" and the other "Magic." It seemed as if when I walked by them I was entering a portal.

Once inside, you knew you had arrived in a special place. There were always the scents of incense and sage, music playing, and activity happening either on the phone or on the computers reaching out to the Universe sharing the Strategic Attraction™ message. In other words, there was always good energy flowing and lots of it!

There is no mistake on how important the "where" is when doing a process such as this. While the actual "how to" of the Kitchen Table Planning session is quite unique, attention to the environment for the session is essential.

First, the *tools* that are used in this process are large white foam boards and lots of colorful sticky notes, and many fun, bright, colorful markers. These tools really help to develop a strategy or project utilizing our creative sides to balance out the process.

Next, and before we actually began, we always *created the space* for the optimum process. Burning sage and incense, setting intentions, and "BEE-ing" for the time together, and possibly having music like *Medicine Woman* by Medwyn Goodall playing or something by Alanis Morissette, depending! And of course the official "SACAT," Jan's adored kitty, Amanda, would always be present. The King Bee, Alan, would sometimes be a part of the sessions, and sometimes he would be happily buzzing on his computer in the next room, or even out at the gym working out. Wherever Alan is physically, he is a catalyst and always holds a huge space for transformation. Whatever the combination, it always seemed perfect.

Then we would proceed to put up ideas on the topic we were focusing on—be that the SACAT coaching program, teleclasses, retreats, book ideas, or other project ideas. We would start with the topic ideas and then add the steps.

What I so admired and literally was amazed by was the process of going with the natural timing of it all. After being trained inside of corporations for over twenty years, my experience of meetings was that they did not get reset because it didn't feel like time to have them. Jan has helped me to see the value of allowing the information to emerge organically, not to push, and not to rush it. I honor this about Jan and the way she has created, and continues to create, her business. My corporate training had ingrained in me the idea to always stay busy, always do something to keep things moving. My "ah-ha moment" came at one of the Kitchen Table sessions when I was retrained in the understanding of letting things happen in perfect timing rather than attempting to push and force an outcome to happen.

The SACAT program was created using the Kitchen Table Planning Process. Jan, Alan, and I would spend hours putting up ideas, rearranging them, putting them in a sequence, and deciding what was next on the "to be" and on the "to be done" lists to create the program.

And this is how the SACAT program was designed and developed! The initial group of four, around that kitchen table, bringing into reality the ideas, the concepts, and the sequence of the pieces that began as sticky notes in the Kitchen Table Planning Process.

And like any other beginning program, it was just that—only the beginning.

This process is now used extensively in my business and with my clients to provide clarity and to have a visual tool that seems to appeal to my perfect clients. No surprise! It has helped me to clarify how I want to structure my new company, i-*SHIFT* Now! I now provide coaching and transformational learning programs for individuals and teams to create connections and empower possibility. Kitchen tables can help to manifest magic. Try it out and see what you can cook up!

PATTY WALTERS, HOUSTON, TX, LICENSED AND CERTIFIED MASTER STRATEGIC ATTRACTION™ COACH/ FOUNDER AND HEAD COACH, I-*SHIFT* NOW!

Chapter TWO

Speaking and Sharing from the Heart

"From the moment you enter a room or walk to the stage, people pick up signals about you and your competence. No matter how uncomfortable you feel, make a conscious decision to exhibit easy confidence and enjoyment of speaking." —DEBORAH SHAMES/DAVID BOOTH, ELOQUI™

WE humans speak in a way that projects how we feel about ourselves to the outside world whether we know it or not. The signal we send is similar to a radio wave that is felt or sensed by others that are in tune with our message. The energetic quality of our BEE-ing, our voice, our presence, has the power to attract or repel, to open or close, to give or receive, to constrict or expand. In a perfect world, we want our speaking to convey what is most important to us through our words, gestures, posture, and tone of our voice, and to present an image of who we are to the world.

It takes years of practice of speaking to groups or audiences to be able to speak in a compelling way that opens both our hearts and the heart of each person in the room—this is what we call speaking and sharing from your heart.

Take a lesson from cats. A cat "speaks" all of the time. Her meow says volumes—feed me, love me, let me go outside. Her tail is also a clue. If you do something she likes, her tail is soft and moves gently from side to side. If a dog walks into the room, her tail goes stiff and points straight up. If you ignore a cat, she will eventually walk away and find a comfortable nesting spot. If you attempt to convince a cat to come sit on your lap, then she often ignores your pleas unless it absolutely suits her. In other words, cats talk with audible and physical language expressions that let you know exactly what they want.

Cats know who they are. They don't walk around wondering if they will be arrogant, demanding, or secure in themselves today. They don't have doubts about whether they will get what they want. They are who they are every day—*a cat!*

You can develop the ability to open your heart and share the love that you feel with others by using the four steps of your BEE-ing Attraction Plan to identify what is important to you. People that you have in your life serve as models of what you want to attract, or perhaps help you to clarify what you definitely don't want. When you begin to notice the subtle qualities, characteristics, and attributes of others, you are tuning in to what is most important to you. You start by seeing the magnificence in another person as something that you desire to have in your own life, and you see that this quality or characteristic is something you want in your customer base or in your closest relationships. Realize that these people you are attracting, who demonstrate the desired traits or qualities, are people that you attracted—therefore, you must also have that quality inside of you to have noticed it in them!

When you realize who you are is also represented in your attraction plan, then you will find it easier to speak from your heart, from your power, and from what makes you tick because by the very nature of the process, you are defining *you.*

JAN H. STRINGER *and* ALAN HICKMAN

"The process we were taught helps me to learn more about myself, what I want and like at the moment—and that is an important part! I am constantly changing, and that includes my wants, values, and understanding of who I am." —CRAIG

Now you have the opportunity to practice speaking from the heart in every interaction you have with people in your business and community. Consider that each conversation you have is a chance to

- be the person that you desire to be and how you desire to be seen by others;
- make a difference for every person you speak to in every interaction;
- practice speaking powerfully, which ultimately empowers and energizes you;
- build confidence internally in your speaking ability.

Whether you are just starting a business, expanding one, or taking it to the next level—speaking is an essential part because you are the main attraction. People want to do business with people that are confident, passionate and provide value to others. If you are someone who is speaking and sharing from your heart, your BEE-ing Attraction Plan would include qualities, characteristics, and attributes like:

- speaks from their heart;
- makes a difference in the world from their service;
- exudes confidence;
- is passionate about their business and product;
- cares about others.

Speaking to Your Board of Directors

Most entrepreneurs and small business owners don't have a Board of Directors because frankly they are just too small. However, you can create a similar group that will provide a space of accountability, a place to brainstorm, and a nonjudgmental community to share about your needs in running a business. Your Board of Directors can be a one-time opportunity or a group that you relate to as if they were in your company.

The point is that when you are speaking to any group, imagine that they *are* your Board of Directors, and practice sharing in the same way as if they were going to make decisions based on what you are saying.

Invoke Feeling in Others with Your Sharing

One day Jan went to a new businesswomen's networking group in her new home town. She had been to many events like that before she moved to her new community and was excited to meet local businesswomen. Feeling a little uncomfortable before she arrived, she called a good friend and told her about her nervousness. During the conversation with her friend, she created who she would BEE during the luncheon before she arrived in the room. Jan's friend helped her to remember how important it is to be clear about her BEE-ing as an important step in connecting to her heart, even when she was nervous about meeting the new people. The BEE-ing she created for herself was, *"Who I am BEE-ing is a successful businesswoman and author causing hearts to open and relationships to blossom."* When she arrived at the door, she was feeling the powerful BEE-ing as she entered the room. To Jan's delight the room was filled with women who were just like her—open, heartfelt, and caring.

During the meeting each person was called to go to the front of the room and hold the microphone to introduce themselves. In other such groups, most people stood up quickly next to their chair and said their name and business name. However, this group seemed more intimate and *hearts* were definitely open. As Jan's turn came, she walked to the front of the room with the intention of being recognized as a professional speaker (which she had trained to be for many years) and without any forethought of what she would say, allowed her heart to open as she started to speak. She began by sharing with her imagined Board of Directors how fortunate she felt to be included in the group of such powerful businesswomen because she was new in town and hadn't had the opportunity to attend any other gatherings of this kind. She felt moved as she shared her true feelings and could feel the softness of tears around her eyes.

After the luncheon, one of the group members thanked her for the heartfelt sharing, and that she recognized how challenging it can be to open your heart when speaking to a group of strangers. Jan felt acknowledged by the comment, and also it validated what she had created in her BEE-ing before the event.

Use Visualization to Prepare for Speaking to a Group or Audience

Imagine yourself on a stage with an audience of millions tuning in to hear what you are saying. Think of how you want to make every word count and affect those who are listening so they clearly understand your message. Remember that you want to hold their attention and have them be interested in you and enamored by what you are telling them.

Your Powerful Speaking is a Result of Others Listening to You!

When people speak, the best gift that you can give to them is your full attention and presence. Let them see you listening to their words carefully, or if you are on the telephone, practice listening intently to the other person on the other end of the call. By all means, turn off your TV and your computer screen as they speak to you. When you notice that the person on the other end of the telephone seems to be droning on in a lengthy explanation, notice whether or not you are actually listening and giving them the attention they deserve. When you notice that you have drifted off during conversation, practice bringing your attention fully to the other person. Chances are that the Chatty Kathy on the other end will be able to slow down long enough to take a breath and you can interject a comment.

When your full attention is given, experience the reward you will receive if you listen to every word they are speaking as being *brilliant*. Hear their words as *gold nuggets*, the answer to your prayers and as if they were sharing the very words that will save your life or the life of your family. Give them your fullest attention.

Practice Listening to Bring Out the Best in Others

Imagine that someone is telling you the secrets of ultimate financial success; think of how you would not want to miss a single word that person is telling you. Imagine yourself listening to someone who is about to share with you the key to eternal happiness and good health; you would be hanging on their every word, would you not? Practice active listening; don't wait for the other person to be done talking just so you can speak. Open your ears and listen to every word they are saying.

> *The key to successful listening is developing your ability to both speak from your heart and to listen with all of your heart.*

The key to successful listening is developing your ability to both speak from your heart and to listen with all of your heart. The heart has no judgments. The heart has no fear. The heart has only love to share with others. When we are speaking from a place that is heartcentered, then we will attract more relationships that are in harmony with our true nature and that will feel more satisfying and fulfilling to participate in.

In the book, *Attracting Perfect Customers: The Power of Strategic*

JAN H. STRINGER *and* ALAN HICKMAN

Synchronicity, marketing was defined as the building of relationships. In this book, this marketing concept is expanded to include building relationships which are heartcentered that feel good to you.

To become a powerful speaker you first have to become a good listener. Practice being a good listener any time someone is speaking to you. If you are at a meeting or gathering, give the speaker your undivided attention. When you are greeting people before the meeting, give them the gift of being listened to with your whole heart and attention.

Chances are when it is your turn to take the speaker's microphone you will have an attentive audience that wants to hear what you have to say. When people are listening to you with full attention eloquent words will flow easily, and you can speak from your heart in a way that allows you to connect with the audience.

Powerful Speaking with a Partner

A pair or couple that is presenting together can be very powerful and it can also be disastrous! Speaking with a partner takes lots of dedication, practice, and training to be able to communicate in tandem so that each person can be heard equally and powerfully.

Advanced planning and practice is essential to prepare properly. BEE-ing ready before the big day is essential. Jan and Alan worked with Speaking Coaches (*see Eloqui in the Resource section*) to help them learn some of the basic techniques and to learn how to pass the presentation back and forth between the two of them successfully. One tip that was especially helpful was when one partner was speaking, the other partner listened. In this situation, your ability to listen is very important; the partner that is listening is also giving their full attention to the speaking partner by looking at them directly and intently when they are speaking. By casting their gaze on the speaking partner, the audience also gave their attention to the speaker. Also, the listening partner was waiting for his or her cue to begin speaking—without which both partners begin speaking over each other and actually go into a power struggle, which is easily detected by the audience.

This is why prior training and practice is essential if you are planning to speak with a partner. This practice of listening to another person speak can be implemented in every situation. When your customers or clients are speaking to you, give them your full attention and you will see the dramatic effect that listening provides. Jan and Alan practice this exercise even when they are in a social setting or visiting with each other over dinner.

Rules of Improvisation

Presentation Coach and Improv Specialist, Patty Walters, (*see Coaches in Resource section*) shares these four Improv Tools, as a way to have fun while presenting with your partner. These rules are also very effective to remember and apply with any relationship, partner, spouse, or friendship.

Rule # 1 - **Make everyone right**

Consider that everyone is right and their perspective has value even if it doesn't match your beliefs. After your partner speaks, practices saying, "Yes and..." then add what you are going to say. If you say, "Yes, but..." you have essentially negated everything your partner just said and therefore makes you both look bad.

Rule # 2 - **Be a character of your authentic self**

Step onto the stage of life as a character of your authentic self; become a characterization of yourself. For example: Patty created a character called "Flo" who works at the Tastee Freeze. In this character she gets to exaggerate a fun part of herself, which may not be expressed every day, and is a depiction of one aspect of her personality. In this character, you create a "self," which is exactly what happens when you create your BEE-ing with your BEE-ing Attraction Plan.

Rule #3 - **Be in the moment**

There you are on stage and you forget the words you were about to say. Your partner who is listening attentively to you realizes the situation and picks up with the story or words as if he or she knew exactly what you were going to say. This is an example of BEE-ing in the moment. Times like these can become fun and entertaining when you relax and just flow with what is happening in the moment rather than trying to say the perfect or right thing.

Rule #4 - **Make your partner look brilliant**

Regardless of what your partner says, regardless of how stupid you think his or her words might be, regardless of whether the script is being followed—make your partner look brilliant after everything they say. After Alan shares something to the audience, Jan will say "Exactly." or "That's Perfect, Alan." or "You are brilliant!" Then she can add anything she wants to his comments and he looks brilliant and so does she.

Rule #4 is especially effective with a team of people and works beautifully to develop trust and synergy in the team experience.

"Wow, your words are so lovely and eloquent and inspiring! I was affected and amazed at how Jan and Alan brought the love they share for each other to the call, how they found each other using the process; their energy in sharing it far deepened my understanding." —LEILA

If you are sharing from your heart, some of the items on your BEE-ing Attraction Plan, which you'll learn to create in Part Two, would be:
- they demonstrate that they love themselves through their words, actions and presentation;
- they speak confidently to individuals and groups;

- they practice listening intently to others;
- they open their hearts when addressing groups or individuals;
- they see every opportunity as a place to practice sharing from their heart;
- they do the work it takes to become an effective speaker.

CUSTOMER STORY

My Defining Moment: Speaking and Sharing from My Heart
BY PATTY WALTERS

There I stood on the stage of an auditorium in Houston, Texas, filled with business people, all looking and listening to what I had to say. What I had to say was to lead a workshop on Strategic Attraction™. The audience was a women's business organization that had asked me to present at this particular meeting. I had even "auditioned" with the program committee a few months before. It was a big deal for me!

What the audience didn't know about that workshop was that it turned out to be a defining moment for me. In that moment in time I was making a decision that would change the course of my life. I had taken a part-time contract, which would become a full-time contract in a few months with my former employer. This was, of course, because of the money, and that I knew the people I would be working with. Then there was this other part of me really wanting to pursue my coaching and training development business. The decision came as I was talking about the Law of Attraction, of becoming a lighthouse instead of a searchlight, and of getting to say what is perfect for us in any moment. In that moment, I realized what was perfect for me. There I was—BEE-ing on stage, dressed in my perfect speaking outfit, confident, calm, feeling very powerful, having fun, and speaking to a warm, attentive audience. I remember the words going through my head: "I can never get *this* working inside of a company!"

That afternoon, at the official PerfectCustomers, Inc. world headquarters, which was then located in Houston, Jan was helping me with the choice. She held out two hands. She said in one hand is the coaching and training work, in the other the contract work. You choose, she said. It didn't take long for me to realize that the choice for me was really quite clear. I was to follow my heart, my intuition, my desire, my passion. Coaching and training was it. I made a call that afternoon to the manager of the contract to let her know that I could not continue on the contract. While it wasn't hard to do, it was a bit daunting, a huge relief, and a bit scary and exciting, all at the same time.

In the months that followed, I became quite involved with PerfectCustomers, Inc. in developing the Strategic Attraction™ Coaches Academy of Training (SACAT). Working with Jan at the "kitchen table" at the world headquarters, with white boards and sticky notes (a highly recommended planning tool, by the way!) proved to be the foundation for what was to become a program and a way of life. It included a mastery level of training, many coaching opportunities, and transforming lives through the power of BEE-ing more of who we are meant to be and designing lives around what makes us tick. For me, the thing that made me tick was the freedom to be me; to be the lighthearted, flowing, and fun-spirited being that I knew I was here to fully express.

As I began to design my life more around what made me tick, I also became involved in a stage production with a theater company in Houston. I became part of a show production called *Bawdy Broads Broadway Bound*! Not only did we create, produce, and perform several shows in Houston, but we also traveled to New York City to perform at the Sage Theater. I had experiences of BEE-ing on stage, of creating characters, of singing to an audience (which I had believed all of my life could never happen), of speaking to many groups of people, of having my own business, of having a rich and powerful spiritual life and community, of being a part of a growing coaching community, and my daily experiences with busting loose from all the beliefs that I had created all of my life to keep me from my full expression.

I've now attracted and become a faculty member at the Executive Coaching Institute at the University of Houston. I'm also a sought-after speaker, and have developed individual and team coaching programs to transform relationships by changing ourselves, our beliefs, and our communications. My seminars, "TeamSHIFT" and "Life is better with a BOA," are gaining popularity. My coaching programs and seminars all include the Strategic Attraction™ Planning process. My individual coaching practice is growing and I am earning certification as a coach through the International Association of Coaching. And of course, I had the honor of adding my story to this *BEE-ing Attraction* book. And in each moment it's a choice of BEE-ing fully present with what makes me tick. And what makes me tick has evolved as well. What makes me tick today is BEE-ing Bold, Outrageous, and Authentic.

PATTY WALTERS, HOUSTON, TX, LICENSED AND CERTIFIED MASTER STRATEGIC ATTRACTION™ COACH/ FOUNDER AND HEAD COACH, I-*SHIFT* NOW!

Chapter THREE

What Makes You Tick?

"What makes me tick is working with people to discover a deeper connection to create heart-centered lives and businesses." —JAN H. STRINGER

AFTER years of working with people to get in touch with what is most important to them in the world, what they are passionate about, what their core purpose is, their Soul's Title, what makes them tick—Jan had an ah-ha moment for herself! Her moment might seem to be obvious to someone else; however, to her what was revealed in that instant is truly what makes her tick.

Jan describes her experience:

"I was speaking with our publisher at Wyatt-MacKenzie, Nancy Cleary. Nancy had offered to review the progress of this manuscript to see what needed to happen next. Before I sent it to her to review, I spent over twelve hours implementing changes suggested by my editor, redrafting chapters, moving the sequence around, and so on. Then I sent it out to Nancy to take a look. When we spoke again to discuss her findings, Nancy was very quiet and not her normal, bubbly self. I felt a bit uneasy inside and was starting to fear what I might hear about my writing. I noticed as Nancy spoke that I felt defensive inside and a bit of anger rose up. I bit my

lip to keep from saying something sharp in retort. When I noticed my emotions I knew this was a signal that something was not feeling right to me. I heard the suggestions being made but was internally rejecting them. Finally I spoke up in as polite a manner as I could muster, saying that there was something missing in this conversation.

What blurted out were my true feelings that had never been fully expressed until this book was attempting to emerge—the carrying forth of our teachings on a deeper level. Later after we hung up, I realized that I had just birthed my tick, and the essence of this second book—stories that illuminate the work I've done with our clients! It's the BEE-ing in action. I chuckled to myself, which is something I have come to recognize as a sign that the truth has been revealed, that after all of these years I had finally come to truly understand, and appreciate, my own true purpose.

I realized when I started the business and the first book was written, it was all about sales and marketing; however, what was inside of me now was the desire to work with people in a deeper, more heart-centered way. It explains why every 'advanced-level' program focused on what makes a person tick, what makes their heart sing."

The nature of determining your tick is revealed to you over time and cannot be forced or pushed out. It is something that only you can say is *your* tick. While others can listen and help you decipher what is most important to you, only you know what resides in the core of you.

> "Doing the BEE-ing Attraction Plan helps me align my compass to my North Star." —SHARON

The BEE-ing Attraction Plan, and all of the work that we have taught over the years, revolved around the importance of understanding what makes a person tick. Business owners have often stepped over the fact that what makes the best client relationship is when you are clear about what makes you tick. The Law of Attraction helps you to understand that our perfect relationships tick to the same beat—like attracts like—and you can probably confirm that your best relationships are the ones that share this common purpose.

Take for example, Bill, senior partner in a new firm. Bill had invited our company to work with them in creating a BEE-ing Attraction Plan for their new partnership. When the process came to the part of the plan about what makes their perfect client tick, Bill stopped the discussion and set his pen down.

He looked up and said, "For the last two weeks that I have been anticipating this meeting, I have been dreading this appointment! Every time the phone rings, before I pick it up, I say to myself—is this a perfect client or am I going to have to get rid of them?"

"Then the other day Grouchy called." He explained that Grouchy was one of his longest standing clients that started working with Bill when he started in business twenty years ago. They nicknamed him "Grouchy" because he always had a doom-and-gloom attitude. He always said something negative and everyone in the office joked about him when he called and avoided answering his calls. Then Bill went on to say that Grouchy had called and asked to cash in a part of an investment in the amount of fifty thousand dollars. Bill had kidded him saying, "Why do *you* need fifty thousand dollars?" Then the client explained that he had one kid getting married, one starting college, and one who needed to buy a car.

At this point in the conversation, Jan interrupted Bill and said she would like to ask him a question. Jan asked, "Bill, if you had to say what makes Grouchy tick, what would you say?" Bill said, "Oh, I have never asked him such a thing." Jan said, "Well, if you had to guess, what would you say?"

Bill paused to reflect on the question and then said, "This man is someone who cares about his family and that is why he invested his money—he wanted his family to have it better than when he was growing up."

Jan said, "Great! Bill, seeing that about him, what would you now say makes you tick?"

Bill got this deer-in-the-headlights-look. He said, "I would say what makes me tick is building a legacy for my family–just like Grouchy!" Everyone at the table seemed amazed because as Bill had recognized that there was a deeper connection, one of the partners said, "I will never think of him as Grouchy anymore. I will only think of him as a legacy builder."

Jan asked Bill what else had he seen for himself in this example. He said, "I just realized that after all of these years of doing business with Grouchy, I thought I stayed with him just because our relationship was financially lucrative for me. What I just realized is that what kept our relationship going over the last twenty years is that we both tick to the same thing!"

When you get to the bottom of your tick, it always seems to be an ah-ha moment. While everyone may experience it in a different way, some of the reactions that you might have when you truly get to your tick are:
- feeling scared;
- feeling tickled;
- laughing out loud and wanting to cry at the same time;
- smiling from ear to ear;
- radiating light from your face;
- feeling humbled.

What makes you tick is the most important thing that you can discover and is the centerpiece around which a heart-centered business develops. In essence, it is the heart of the business because it comes from the heart and soul of you!

"I took to heart all the enlightened marketing guidance you gave me in the BEE-ing Attraction class, and I totally got what makes me tick. I was so excited by this clarity that I wrote it on my business cards and

added it to my web site. However, the most powerful piece for me was when I created a thirty-second marketing piece from what makes me tick and combined it with the powerful metaphor you shared with me. It expressed exactly what I do so powerfully that, when I stood up and shared, everybody's mouth dropped. It set a whole new standard for thirty-second marketing pieces, and after the lunch people were flocking to my booth."
—MELODY

CUSTOMER STORY

Holding Myself Back...Nevermore!
BY SUZY GIRAUD

As I began the whole process of signing up for the Strategic Attraction™ Class, I noticed how smart and smug and confident I was to create this document with just the right words to attract my perfect clients. After all, I had successfully implemented this plan for many previous and past clients, myself included. So I signed up for the Mini-BEE teleclass with Alan, and as the sessions rolled on and I was able to very smartly and corporate-like glide my way through, I reached a snag...*what makes Suzy tick?*

Whatever could he mean, as the silence on the community call was all ears to me! I couldn't drop into this question *until* I emotionally, all at once, took it out of my brain and into my heart...I answered, "Play." The word itself just stood out in the field of energy waiting for a connection. So I began to connect with this word and my process of holding myself back was changed forever.

For the longest time, since my leaving a career with a prestigious title and influence, I have been in a no-go zone. A "no-go zone" is for me, after lots of consideration, a place where you always have something—always—to keep you from your dream. For me it always took the form of...A New Beginning. So this was the manner in which I conducted my life. And then along came a message from my Spirit: You need and want to ask Jan Stringer to coach you. *What?* I questioned. Somehow I knew this was to be true and I followed up on an intuitive nudge and placed a call to Jan.

Our connection did not occur at first, but shortly thereafter. When we did start working together we connected on a heart and soul level, which made our work much more enjoyable.

The whole encompassing process of BEE-ing was the click that unlocked the door of my enthusiasm, excitement, and heart.

When I became connected to what makes me tick and who I would be BEE-ing to have what I wanted to attract, it anchored my dream of Wowieekazowiee Creative Camps! No more holding Suzy back. My passion was released, flooded, and anchored in my heart. This was all created in the energy of play! What a relief as I laughed all the way into, through, and beyond the evolving BEE-ing the business of Wowieekazowiee!

There are still some residues from this time and I still have some very large dazzling distractions; however, for the most part I have focused on the commitment to the vibrant energy that Wowieekazowiee asks me to commit to—the Art of Play. Who I am BEE-ing is attracting people that want to explore their abilities to express their creativity and play.

As they say, a story is a promise, and that's my story.

SUZY GIRAUD, DIRECTOR OF WOWIEEKAZOWIEE CREATIVE CAMPS FOR THE WOW OF YOU! SUZY ARRIVED ON THIS BLUE PLANET TO TEACH, SHARE, AND EXPRESS HER MISSION OF PLAY! A FORMER TEACHER, PUBLISHER OF *IT'S NEWS TO ME*, PRESIDENT OF CREATIVE BONES, AND FOUNDER OF WOWIEEKAZOWIEE, SUZY COACHES ALL GENERATIONS IN THE ART OF LAUGHTER AND ARTISTIC EXPRESSION ALL THE LIVE LONG DAY! SHE RESIDES IN SUNNY CALIFORNIA WITH HER HUSBAND, TWO CHILDREN, FOUR GRANDCHILDREN, AND LOTS OF IMAGINARY PLAYMATES! SUZYG@COX.NET

CUSTOMER STORY

Branding from the Heart: How a Strange Little Question Transformed My Business and My Life

BY JULIA D. STEGE, MFA/STRATEGIC ATTRACTION™ COACH

What makes you tick? It seemed like a pretty strange question when I first heard it on a one hour Perfect Customers tele-class years ago. I didn't know it could transform my life and the life of my customers. After all, what did it mean?

I pondered it for a while. What makes you and your perfect customers tick? Since Law of Attraction says "Like Attracts Like," then my perfect customers are attracted to me because we are alike?

I guess that makes sense, I thought. Though that's not at all what I had learned when I began my career on Madison Avenue. The marketing world talked about targeting an audience and then tailoring everything to them, inundating them with repeated messages. They didn't talk about the business owner or what their life-purpose was. But then again, they didn't know about the Law of Attraction either.

Though a new approach to marketing was being born in my mind, I wanted to put it to the test first. So I determined what made me tick as a first step. I wrote down a list of words that I knew held strong meaning for my life. Words like:
- freedom
- creativity
- love
- magic
- communication
- transformation
- justice
- beauty
- the environment

I lay in bed at night musing over my tick and paid attention to what desires burned at the core of my BEE-ing. Then whenever anyone called me about needing a logo or a web site, I asked them questions like, "What makes you tick? What gets you up in the morning? What keeps you burning the midnight oil? What is your soul purpose? Why are you here?" And I wrote it down.

And guess what they said?

They said words like *freedom*, *creativity*, *beauty*, *love* and *teaching*. "Oh, I like that one," I'd reply, and I wrote that down on my list. "We are simpatico."

This happened often, where either they'd say words I'd already written on my list, or their words would inspire me and touch my heart. Each time my mind got clearer and clearer. What makes me tick really is what makes my perfect customers tick!

What makes me tick really is what makes my perfect customers tick!

About this time someone gave me a Rumi quote. "What you seek is seeking you." When I heard that quote my whole body relaxed. If what I seek (my perfect customers) is seeking me right now, then if I'm authentic in my marketing they will recognize me when they find me. In fact, if I'm hyped or hardsell or trying to sound like someone else, my perfect customers won't recognize me at all.

I looked at my own marketing pieces and realized that there was an element of slickness to them that wasn't truly authentic. One of my colleagues told me that the design didn't reflect my radiance, my energy. That's when I decided to include magical stars coming off the paintbrush in my *Mona Lisa* logo, and put her on a backdrop of my own whimsical landscape drawings.

Though I felt vulnerable, like I was exposing my little kid self to the world, I also knew that vulnerability is authentic, and that is the key to attracting my perfect customers and living my true life's purpose.

JAN H. STRINGER *and* ALAN HICKMAN

When my own logo and marketing pieces changed, the kinds of projects I attracted changed with them. Everyone wanted to talk about the Law of Attraction and how we could imbue their logos and web sites with that magical power.

I created a process for people to explore their true purpose while creating their company brand image, and I called the process *Branding from the Heart*™. I include this process in all of my design projects, marketing classes, and workshops because it is so powerful. It's a great process for creating business and product names, web site addresses, keywords, book titles, and blogging topics that reflect true meaning and promote what we really care about. This is truly the opposite of hype!

Recently I hosted a *Branding from the Heart*™ retreat on a beautiful property in Santa Rosa called Mystic Oak Gardens. I invited a circle of women to come to this cozy setting and share what makes us tick. We all brought good food and we sat in front of the fire drinking tea and sharing our souls. There is nothing as beautiful as a circle of women sharing their life passion, their true purpose, and really being heard. The tears flowed as we touched each other's hearts and acknowledged each other's struggles, our successes, and our dreams.

When the day was drawing to a close we were all uplifted, sharing business cards and hugs. I asked them if they had ever heard anything as compelling as someone sharing what makes them tick. Everyone agreed, yes, it is the most compelling thing.

So why would we not share *that* in our marketing? Let's share our true purpose in our marketing in a way that promotes everything we're up to. That's how we will not only attract our perfect customers, but we will fulfill our life purposes as well. We will attract people who are on the same path, and who need our specific offerings to help them on their way, just as we need their resources to help us on our path.

So I hope you go forth and shine your true self to the world. Use your "Tick Words" in your promotions along with the words that describe your offerings and see how magically attractive your marketing becomes. And who knows, you might notice your life transforming in ways you hadn't yet dreamed.

JULIA D. STEGE IS KNOWN AS THE MAGICAL MARKETER BECAUSE SHE HELPS ENTREPRENEURS ATTRACT PERFECT CUSTOMERS WITH A COMBINATION OF ATTRACTION MARKETING CONSULTING, BEAUTIFUL DESIGNS, AND SOCIAL NETWORKING STRATEGIES. SHE CONTRIBUTES REGULARLY TO THE LAW OF ATTRACTION MARKETING BLOG (LOAMARKETING.BLOGSPOT.COM) AND LEADS TELECLASSES, WEBINARS, AND RETREATS ON *ATTRACTING PERFECT CUSTOMERS ONLINE*, *TELECLASS MAGIC*, AND *BRANDING FROM THE HEART*™. JULIA HOLDS A BFA IN GRAPHIC DESIGN, AN MFA IN MEDIA STUDIES, AND IS A STRATEGIC ATTRACTION™ COACH. GET HER FREE MAGICAL MARKETING TOOLKIT AT WWW.MAGICALMARKETINGTOOLKIT.COM.

Chapter FOUR

Creating Your BEE-ing

"For beings who feel there's more to life than just making honey." —JOHN PENBERTHY, *TO BEE OR NOT TO BEE*

THE concept of *Creating your BEE–ing* can best be understood by the metaphor of a bumblebee.

"According to all known laws of aviation, there is no way that a bee should be able to fly. Its wings are too small to get its fat little body off the ground. The bee of course, flies anyway. Because the bees don't care what humans think is impossible." —*BEE MOVIE*

The fat little bumblebee is the ideal symbol to convey what happens when you are successful in the face of great odds. The bumblebee with its oversized body and small wings is able to fly. The fact that the bumblebee can fly defies logic, and in some ways so does creating your own BEE-ing. In the "Wisdom of Avalon Oracle Cards" the BEE represents luck, industriousness, and sweet victory.

You probably won't find this interpretation of BEE-ing in any book or film about quantum physics or in a study on *the nature of being* in quite the same way. One of the many benefits of the BEE-ing

Attraction Planning process is that it is highly effective in shifting old paradigms that represent who you have been in the past, and who you have to be in order to attract your desires. It is a focus with a powerful belief that you will attract in accordance with your plan (see Part II of the book to create your plan). In other words, when you write down your intentions on the plan, you bring attention to what you want to attract. After you are clear about what you want to attract, then you declare who you have to BEE to attract what you have written on the plan. Clear and focused intentions together with your declaration of BEE-ing are energizing, and other people can sense or feel the signal that is coming from you.

One of the reasons businesses fail is that the owners did not realize the key point of their business success lies in *creating their BEE-ing* first. Many business owners make this common mistake because there is a cultural example that seems to support taking actions first. However, this is the business person's pitfall when they get caught up in the *doing* of their business and end up in an endless cycle of work.

"But hadn't all of them once been entrepreneurs? After all, they had started their business. There must have been a dream that drove them to take such a risk. But, if so, where was the dream now? Why had it faded? Where was the entrepreneur who had started the business? The answer is simple: the entrepreneur had only existed for a moment."
—MICHAEL E. GERBER, *THE E-MYTH REVISITED*

The BEE-ing Attraction Plan is an effective tool to stay present in the act of BEE-ing an entrepreneur, CEO, president, or any other business position. When you have a BEE-ing Attraction Plan, you become more focused on what is important to you and it keeps you on track. It is about taking time to "work on your business rather than in your business" as Michael Gerber points out brilliantly in *The E-Myth Revisited*.

For example, if you say that your business target is to sell one million dollars worth of products this year, you must first step into the BEE-ing of someone who sells one million dollars worth of products this year. Too many times you get excited and step over the first ingredient required to run a business, which is to identify and establish your BEE-ing first!

The BEE-ing Attraction Planning process is about shifting paradigms. You must first become what you want to attract! As you determine what is perfect for you, then your expectations begin to come into alignment or energetic balance. Take Alan, for example. Alan had an exciting ah-ha moment when he realized that his perfect customers wanted him to have what he wanted in his business. Alan said this was the most valuable realization in the whole planning process for him, as if for the first time he became aware that his perfect customers would also want him to earn a six-figure income, drive a nice car, and go on vacations every year. Before this insightful moment, he thought that adding these kinds of wishes to his plan sounded vain and self-centered. However, by adding his desires to his plan, he is be able to BEE what is required to attract the very things he says he wants to have. Alan had a paradigm shift when he saw the world in a different way, and this produced a new way for him to BEE in the world. This is what we call *establishing BEE-ing*.

The creation of your BEE-ing is like the "punch line" of your BEE-ing Attraction Plan, which becomes clear in the fourth part. If you have created a Strategic Attraction™ Plan before, perhaps you remember when you came to Part 4 of the plan, which asks, "Who do I get to BEE to attract what I say I want?" or, "What is there for me to improve to BEE more attractive?" Most people hear these questions and their first instinct is to write down all of the things that they need to start "doing" right away to improve.

Instead, the BEE-ing Attraction Plan is a four-step process in who you get to "BEE" in the world to have everything that you say that you want to attract. When we are applying *attraction together with BEE-ing*, you learn that to *attract* a "perfect customer," a "perfect mate" or any other relationship type that you desire to attract, you must first *become* who you say you are and what you say you want. In essence, you must first become your own perfect customer or your perfect relationship.

"Following the Mini-'Bee' class today, I noticed that the anxieties and darkness that had been swallowing me all week had dissipated. My thoughts previously had been, "I don't know who I am. I never have." After Alan suggested to me that what really was true is that I was actually all of what I had been trying to copy and mimic throughout my life. The qualities that impressed me in others were in reality resonating within me. I tried that on. The anxiety left. I was reminded of a lecture I heard years ago by a professor of philosophy. He introduced me to a new thought that anger and other negative emotions are results of living a lie. Identify the lie and the negative emotion goes away. It seems that's exactly what happened to me today. The lie I was living was I don't know who I am. As soon as I let go of that untruth and admitted that I really am all of those wonderful qualities I saw in others, there was no more negativity. Big wow!" —JUDY

Who are you BEE-ing today? This is a simple question. Answering it can actually shift your BEE-ing into a new place when you ask yourself the question, and create who you are BEE-ing, each day. By looking at your BEE-ing Attraction Plan you can see all of the things that you want to attract, and the fun part is to create who you get to BEE to attract what you have written on the plan. In Part 4 of the BEE-ing Attraction Plan you declare your BEE-ing. You ask yourself: *Who do I have to BEE to attract what I say I want?*

For example, participants in one of the training classes answered this part of the plan by giving their BEE-ing a title:

- Mary said, "Who I am BEE-ing is Queen of Clarity and Purpose."
- Michael said, "Who I am BEE-ing is bold, outrageous, and unstoppable."
- Gregg said, "Who I am BEE-ing is Exuberant Marketing Magician."

As you can see from their answers, when the opportunity was given to each person to be creative and imaginative—they had fun developing an answer. Creating their BEE-ing got each of them out of the box and shifted them into a new place within themselves.

In this part of the plan, you will create a title of someone who accomplishes everything you have said you want in the previous parts of the plan. In other words, it encompasses the qualities, characteristics, and attributes of your perfect relationships, what makes you tick, and what you want your perfect customers to expect of you. Let's say your answers in Part 3 of your plan, which complete the phrase *I want my Perfect Customers to expect me,* are the following:

- to take four vacations a year;
- to have a million-dollar business;
- to have my perfect office space;
- to earn a thousand dollars per day;
- to live a balanced life doing what I love;
- to have a business that I love using the power of the Internet.

You would imagine who you have to BEE to accomplish what you have written or who you would have to BEE to attract what you say you want. For example, Jan created this as her BEE-ing for her plan:

"Who I am BEE-ing is: I am the Savvy Goddess of Business energizing a new world." Jan said, "This statement puts a bow on everything for me. It's fun and empowering to me. When I declare it out loud, people smile or laugh at the lighthearted fun it inspires."

Whatever you desire in your life is going to happen in relationship to who you are BEE-ing about what you desire. So if you want to BEE someone who loves what you do and to attract customers as a result of your passion, ask yourself; "What would be the title of someone who is BEE-ing what I have written on my plan?" In other words, who do you get to BEE to attract what you say you want and what you have written on your plan? What is your title? In this example, your title is the same as your BEE-ing.

Here are additional examples of titles or who you might BEE to attract what you have written on your plan—the possible titles of your BEE-ing are only limited by your imagination.

- King of Clarity
- Colorful Goddess of Insights
- Spirit Employed
- Destroyer of Dysfunction
- Chief Officer of Clarity and Purpose
- Master of Balanced Living
- The Listening Teacher
- A Million-Dollar Hottie
- An Unstoppable, Deliberate Attractor

One way to know if you have gotten to the *truth of your BEE-ing* is laughter. When you get to the heart of your BEE-ing, it makes you and others laugh with delight.

Your BEE-ing can change on a moment-to-moment basis. Your BEE-ing is distinct from what makes you tick, which will remain constant for the most part. However, as you create a BEE-ing title, it can change to match your mood or your playful spirit. Regardless of how you are feeling before your creation, it always alters something inside of you. If you are in a funk or your day is not going 100 percent the way you want it to go, take a moment and "create your BEE-ing"; it will open your heart and everything into a new more positive direction.

JAN H. STRINGER *and* ALAN HICKMAN

You might be asking, "Can creating a BEE-ing title really alter my emotions?" Or wondering whether declaring your statement really makes a difference. The answer is, *yes*! Your declaration is part of the magic that comes forth from your BEE-ing. When you create your BEE-ing, you have to reach for another state of mind. It causes you to turn your negative energy into another direction that feels better to you. When you feel good, you will exude that good feeling vibe and that is what your perfect customers really want from you in the first place. Even in the midst of disorganization or a "dazzling distraction," you can stop for a moment and step into your BEE-ing; it informs you of a more powerful place from which to assess the situation that is before you. It's a fun way for you to get in touch with *you*. People want to be with what's important to *you*, not your stuff. People are more attracted to your passion and authenticity than your seriousness or businesslike manner.

Who are you BEE-ing? What is your title? Here are few more ideas:

- I am BEE-ing Joy.
- I am BEE-ing Patient.
- I am BEE-ing Grateful.
- I am BEE-ing Happy.
- I am BEE-ing Harmonious.
- I am BEE-ing a Savvy Business Person.

In the groundbreaking movie *What the Bleep Do We Know!?* released in February 2004, fourteen scientists and mystics explore the worlds of quantum physics, neurology, and molecular biology in relation to the spheres of spirituality and metaphysics. In the movie, Dr. Joe Dispenza shares about how he starts the day by examining "Who am I going to be today? What would I like to project myself to be? What is the greatest ideal of me that I could be?" This movie was one of the first released that gives people the possibility of explaining why thoughts matter.

"It is the best attempt I have seen to move from the quantum field to the biological level. It is a great beginning and it begins to pose some very important questions. How do we see the effects of thought in our lives?"
—JOE DISPENZA

Since the release of this film, many have other observations about the importance of BEE-ing and the impact of the thoughts that people think, such as in the film *The Secret,* which helped this ancient wisdom of the Law of Attraction to reach critical mass.

The art of establishing BEE-ing dates back to ancient times and can be substantiated through quantum physics. The bottomline is that you are what you think, and you attract in direct correlation to who you are BEE-ing about what you think. Here are a few suggestions for you to assist in establishing your BEE-ing:

1. Create your BEE-ing daily rather than defaulting to how you are feeling when you are first awake in the morning. Start with a daily breathing and meditation practice to clear your energy chakras and to connect with your energetic source.

2. Step into the BEE-ing of the day the same way as if you are writing your script for the day. Post your BEE-ing in writing somewhere you can see it during the day like on your computer or a mirror.

3. Have fun and keep it lighthearted—this is actually the only way to create your BEE-ing—from a good attitude.

4. Look over your plan, then make a few additions to your BEE-ing Attraction Plan. Next, pick something that you have written, yet have not yet manifested such as: *BEE-ing the owner of a business that is earning one hundred thousand dollars in annual sales.* For the rest of your day, BEE someone who is the owner of a business earning one hundred thousand dollars in annual sales. See what doors open for you!

JAN H. STRINGER *and* ALAN HICKMAN

5. Set your goals for the day after you have connected to the energy of your BEE-ing; notice the increase of life force and energy present for you in the moment. (See chapter 15 for more on Setting Goals in the Energy of BEE-ing.)

6. Declare your BEE-ing and goals to another person. When you declare your daily BEE-ing to another person, it becomes more powerful within you. It strengthens your ability to resist the dazzling distractions of the day.

Who are you BEE-ing during difficult times?

There will be times when you are effectively *BEE-ing who you need to be in order to fulfill what makes you tick and what you want to attract*. At other times, you may feel unrecognized for who you "truly" are by others and even by yourself.

For instance, Nan is working on creating her own business, and knows through her BEE-ing Attraction Planning that this is in alignment with her greatest desires. She intellectually understands the importance to feel abundant and as though this business is going to take off at some point; however, as the bills pile up, it gets difficult to feel the success in her heart. To make matters worse, when she goes home to visit with her parents, they are skeptical of what she is doing. They remind her constantly that she is not creating a solid income at this point in time, and perhaps she should look for a more traditional job that pays a steady wage and gives benefits.

We asked Nan who she thought she was BEE-ing when she appeared on her family's front doorstep. She told us she felt a lack of self-confidence, like a little girl about to be reprimanded and told she was being irresponsible. Clearly, when she was feeling like a child, she was not going to radiate business success, and the way she was feeling was also going to make her parents feel protective and judgmental. It also points out that Nan has some energetic clearing work that needs to be done around who she is BEE-ing as an adult and who she is when around her parents. When a situation keeps occurring such as this one, Nan would want to add to her BEE-ing Attraction Plan something to the effect of:

What I want my perfect customers (or family) to expect of me (Part 3)
- is to clear my childhood issues and be responsible for who I am as an adult;
- is to stop blaming my parents and take ownership of my own life by being responsible;
- is to do the energetic healing work that I require to heal my unresolved emotional issues with my parents.

On Nan's Part 4 of the BEE-ing Attraction Plan, she would write:
Who I am BEE-ing to attract what I say I want is
- Cleared of my childhood issues and a 100 percent responsible adult.
- Author of my successful life.
- Appreciative of my family and friends.

Who would you prefer to BEE?

Alan gave an example of a client named Becky, who had overcome great financial issues. Becky had lost her business partner in a sudden airplane crash, which left her emotionally distraught, and her business went bankrupt. She even lost her home and had to live with her relatives. One day in the middle of her despair, she thought about how in the past she had created a BEE-ing Attraction Plan. She took out a piece of paper, even though her inspiration was very low, and wrote a few words on the plan. Looking back now, she sees that in that moment, the Attraction Plan was her declaration of her intention to move out of the predicament she found herself to be in and to create a new way to BEE.

Things began to shift immediately around her new BEE-ing. Becky received a call from someone who spoke about a business opportunity. The friend was persistent. Fortunately, Becky realized that this was actually a business in alignment with her Attraction Plan; she trusted her gut feeling about the opportunity and took action. Her story is a rags-to-riches story because Becky has now become a successful business owner and earned over $500,000 in her first year of business.

You can control your mind and leave the negative talk out of your conversations and thoughts. Create ways to practice making powerful declarations with like-minded and like-hearted friends. Declare your BEE-ing at every opportunity and in every conversation. Your declaration and intentions will turn the worst situations around so that you are ultimately attracting the best in every case.

> *"Now in the moment we ask those questions, our brain begins to send information to the frontal lobe and we begin to rely on past experience to experience a new person or ideal of ourselves. We know from scientific studies that thinking can make new circuits. So when I start out creating my day, I always start out deciding who I am going to be. I remember what the highest ideal of me would be. Can I see everybody as an equal? Can I see everybody without judgment? Can I be patient and understanding? These are all the things I find important in my demonstration of self. Sooner or later I will ultimately become that person."*
> —DR. JOE DISPENZA, *WHAT THE BLEEP DO WE KNOW!?*

Don't give up five minutes before the miracle!

When Jan first started her business she offered teleconferences at no charge to promote her programs, yet up until the last minute she would fret about whether anyone would show up, and what she was going to say. There were many days that, in spite of preparing endlessly, nobody showed up on her calls. Then she put her attention on the phrase, *"Don't give up five minutes before the miracle!"* which in essence gave her a more optimistic way of BEE-ing than she had before. After declaring "Don't give up five minutes before the miracle," she had a surge of attendance. Over twenty people attended, which was a jump in numbers from the previous call where only two people came. Jan's new way of viewing the situation started to pay off as her telephone began to ring with people calling to register for her coaching program. No matter how bad or desperate a situation may look to you, remember that a miracle is waiting to happen just around the corner.

CUSTOMER STORY

The Day I Stepped into the BEE-ing of CEO
BY DOUG UPCHURCH

I will never forget that moment in 2001 when I realized for the very first time how my BEE-ing and doing were connected. Prior to this time, I had experienced a successful career as a manager and executive director within the IT training industry. However, in each of my roles, including executive director, I always worked for someone else, whether it was a board of directors or a manager or owner. In 1999, that all changed when I started my own learning and development business. The only challenge was I didn't figure it out until that moment in 2001. Before we get to that moment, let me give you some context.

In October 1999, I had left a very successful career to start my own learning and development consulting business. Within a month of starting, I was asked by one of the partners I worked with if I could open their first US office. This company was a global learning and development company based in Scotland but with offices in thirty countries. At the time, they had no physical office based in the US yet. So it was truly an honor to be invited to start this journey. Only thing was, it was my business. I had to fund it, find the customers, do the marketing, do the delivery, do the invoicing, you get the idea. I did it all.

No matter how bad or desperate a situation may look to you, remember that a miracle is waiting to happen just around the corner.

So very quickly, I got caught up in all the doing. And in almost every situation, I wanted to make sure I was "doing it right," whatever that meant. Additionally I would take advice from anyone who wanted to give it. My partner, my parents, anyone who I thought knew how to "do it right," I would listen to. And I got a lot of great ideas. In many ways those ideas helped me survive during the first year, along with some very supportive family members. I also found myself doing a lot of IT support work to pay the bills.

But a year into it, I had not achieved the success I had hoped for. I was ready to give up, primarily because I needed a full-time salary again. So I put my resume on a job site thinking that maybe I'll find a good IT training job. In many ways, I felt defeated. A key part of my business was developing more successful and self-aware leaders. I didn't feel like one at this time.

Within two weeks of posting my resume, I got a call from a global company in the IT industry asking if I was still looking for work. They needed someone to fill a Director of IT Training position for their US Business. I jumped at the opportunity, thinking it was my only option. I interviewed with six different people in one day during which I flew out to Silicon Valley and flew back to my home in Texas in 36 hours. One of the questions I asked each of my interviewers was, "How does this company view leadership?" In each case I heard some variation on the theme that it wasn't valued as much as results. This was a message that didn't resonate with me at all. I left thinking I probably wouldn't hear from them again.

Six weeks later, I got the offer for the job. However, I had to ask myself is this really what I want. Did I want to work for a company that held values so contrary to my own regarding leadership? I did some soul searching and talking with my partner and made the decision to decline the offer. I knew that I was either going to be successful at my own business or die trying.

About this time, I had the privilege of meeting Jan Stringer and I hired her as a business advisor and professional coach. I gradually began to learn a unique and powerful concept that has since changed my life. It was the power of understanding my own BEE-ing.

I'll never forget the day I spent with Jan shortly after I turned down this job. We were doing a full-day planning/coaching session and she asked me the question, "Who are you?" I didn't understand at first. I responded with my name and the title I had given myself of Managing Director. "I am the Managing Director of Insights Austin," I said. She challenged me, "So what does that mean?" I proceeded to list a set of responsibilities in my role.

She challenged me again, "I don't want to know what you do, I want to know who you are!" I was stuck. I didn't get it and was starting to feel frustrated. I wasn't "doing it right" and knew that there was something I was missing. I gave in and told Jan, "I don't know who I am. I guess that's the problem."

Jan's next question changed my life.

"Are you the CEO?"

I was taken aback. How could I be the CEO of a one person company? That sounded arrogant and self-important. Surely that's not what she meant. I said, "No, I'm the Managing Director of…" She said, "Stop!" And she picked up a marker and drew a horizontal line on the white board and then drew what looked like a curvy *w* on the line. She asked me if I knew what that was. I didn't. She said "That's your butt, and it's on the line. Is your butt on the line for Insights Austin?" I said, "Absolutely!" She responded with, "Then who you are is a CEO. Your butt is on the line and that's what a CEO is."

Immediately something inside of me switched on. I realized for the first time that I was still operating as the guy working for someone else. I was being a manager, but not a CEO. A CEO has a different level of passion and operates from a different sense of ownership and power. I got it for the first time. It wasn't about "doing the right things." It was about being the right BEE-ing. Not only did this shift my view of myself and my role, but it also shifted my actions. Within three months, I had gained new clients, a new employee, and new distributors to work with my business. Within two years I was appointed the CEO for the North American business unit. And just four years later, my local office was so successful that the global business made the decision to purchase the office from me.

I know that there were two turning points that completely transformed this business. The first was when I said no to a job that didn't align with my values. The second was when I realized that I was no longer reporting to someone, but I was a CEO and my butt was on the line.

DOUG UPCHURCH, LEARNING AND DEVELOPMENT EXECUTIVE. DOUG HAS EIGHTEEN YEARS EXPERIENCE DEVELOPING RELEVANT AND ACCESSIBLE LEARNING. HE IS THE HEAD OF COMMUNITY DEVELOPMENT FOR INSIGHTS, A GLOBAL LEARNING COMPANY. DOUG IS ALSO THE FOUNDER AND CEO OF PRACTICAL SOUL. AS A COACH, INTUITIVE, AND REIKI MASTER TEACHER, HE IS PASSIONATE ABOUT HELPING OTHERS GET RECONNECTED TO THEMSELVES, THEIR NATURAL GIFTS, AND THEIR SOUL.

Chapter FIVE

Why Are You Attracting What You Are Attracting… Again?

"Learning the root causes of your emotions begins with a simple understanding: You are never upset for the reason you think." —PAUL AND LAYNE CUTRIGHT

IN theory, every relationship that you attract is perfect—even the ones that seem to elicit the worst in you. People are drawn to your energy. After you have defined a "perfect fit" relationship for your business, notice who and what results you are attracting. If you are attracting the kind of people that you desire to be with and match what you have written on your attraction plan, then good for you. If you are attracting people and situations that you don't like, it is because the issues within you remain unresolved and are being mirrored back to you by the people around you. For example, a business owner attracts a new client, and after working with them they discover that they have financial problems and can't pay their bill. The business owner hates to admit that they too are strapped for cash flow, and this was primarily why they accepted this new client in the first place. When the business owner first met this potential client, his hunch was that finances could become a problem and he chose to ignore his feelings about it.

Pay attention to the situations that keep happening over and over again. When customers want to know why their marketing strategy does *not* work for them, you can find out by noticing what is happening repeatedly. It is very important to pay attention to the issues that you are attracting over and over again because these people or situations are pointing the way to where you need to do internal clearing and healing work. In this case, it helps to focus on what is *not* happening the way you want life to be, regardless of whether you think that sounds negative. If this bothers you, consider that you are being a detective and are searching for clues to solve a mystery. The simple answer to the mystery of why things don't happen for you or why they do is that you are an energetic BEE-ing who draws to you and repels away from you. It is the cause and effect in your life.

Take personal responsibility for what you attract and for what you *don't* attract. The energy patterns that are within you cause repetitive things or situations to happen; if they are situations that are not to your liking, then the only way that you can shift into a new direction is to focus on what is inside of you that is causing the situation. Being this conscious about your life requires radical personal responsibility rather than being a victim—no exceptions. In essence, these people or situations that you have attracted are your "teachers" because they are showing you what is ready to be healed inside of you.

You can honestly say that all of your relationships and customers are perfect. The people that you attract are helping you to surface what is and what is not perfect and allow you to become more conscious about your goals that are perfect for you. Once you can see that these situations have been drawn to you for a reason, you can begin the work to resolve your emotional issues that bring the repeat patterns into your business and personal relationships.

Usually there are warning signals alerting you to the fact that there is a familiar situation about to happen or that something has just happened that has taken you off guard. For example, Jan notices that she gets angry about something. Alan notices that he starts to defend his position. Something you might say would be "they pushed my buttons" or that person "needs to look at themselves." When you find yourself saying something about another person, it means that *your* switch has been flipped and then an automatic response takes over such as anger, fear, depression, doubt, irritability, and disappointment. If you find yourself saying something about another person as *if* what you are saying is true, then this is another reading on your barometer that *you* have an issue to resolve.

Unfortunately it is never about the other person—regardless of the situation. Every situation that you have attracted is the result of what you have existing in your energetic field.

You are projecting your unresolved issues on your loved ones and customers every time you point your finger at them or blame them for how you are feeling. No exception!

One precaution when working with the BEE-ing Attraction Plan is to be mindful of when an issue shows up in a relationship, whether with a customer or personal relationship, because if their issue is similar to one of your unresolved issues, then you might react and project your issues onto them as if it was *their* problem not yours. Rather than admitting that it is something that you need to look at, you rationalize that you are the authority and the customer must be calling you for the solution. You will attempt to fix the problem for the other person without realizing that this very issue is something inside of you too.

What does it mean to project an issue? Let's say that you have a customer who calls right before an event that they have paid to attend and they say that they are not going to come. Additionally, they begin to tell you their reasons that justify why they will not be participating. You listen to them tell you their list of rationale such as:

- The airline ticket is too expensive.
- They don't want to take off the time to attend.
- They have other priorities to pay attention to.

Then the customer says, "These are not the only reasons that I will not attend, I also want to let you know that I don't like how you have organized the event, and I feel you are not providing what I need to get enough value for me to attend."

Ouch! This is the last thing you wanted to hear as you are planning the event and were counting on every participant. You listen to what the customer is saying and do your best to be objective, attempting to not take it personally as they are speaking.

Now you are at a critical point in your relationship with this customer. Anything you say can and will determine the course your relationship will take! It is also an opportunity to choose whether you will:

a.) own your responsibility;
b.) project your unresolved emotional issues onto the customer.

The best thing you can do is hold back on your desire to bite the customer's head off with a sharp retort, and instead tell the customer that you understand and thank them for calling. When you get off of the phone you can sort out your own feelings and process and clear them without having to engage the customer into your issues. Take a moment to acknowledge the way you handled the situation especially because you did *not* act out your feelings, even with the strong impulse to fire both barrels of your gun at your customer.

You know you are becoming stronger when you can work through your own issues without implicating or without making the other person pay for your emotions. This is an indication that you are on the road to healing your wounds rather than perpetuating them. It takes an emotionally mature person to resist a strong desire to lash out when you are reactivated emotionally inside. If you do act out your emotional upset at one of your customers, more than likely it is in an attempt to try and feel better about yourself. Hopefully you know intellectually that your own healing will *not* occur by lashing out or acting out, which gives you the option to select something that will help you heal in every interaction.

What can you do when your negative or unresolved emotional issues are activated? One rule of thumb in every situation where your strong emotions have been activated, especially when you have the desire to lambast someone else with your hurt feelings, is to step back and walk away for at least twenty-four hours. Get into communication with someone who is trained to support you during these times—a coach, a mentor, a friend—someone who is not going to go into the emotional drama with you and will help you see another perspective. If you call your friend who is untrained or dealing with their own similar issues, this could be a sign that you are not really ready to heal and that you want to perpetuate your story. Griping or complaining and gossiping about a less-than-perfect customer will not alter the situation and more than likely you will continue to attract similar situations like this one again and again until you get to the bottom of your unresolved issue. It is important that you understand that you will continue to attract more situations and people like this until *you have healed your own wounds*.

After you hang up the telephone from the complaining customer, it is best if you sit with the words that have just been spoken to you and do your best to sort through all of the emotions and feelings that are raging in your mind, as well as the hurt that you are experiencing in your heart.

Part of being a conscious business owner is recognizing that your clients are great reflections of you, and they mirror to you who you are BEE-ing and the message you are radiating out to others. When you attract those situations that bring up the areas of your life that are in doubt or unsettled, then it is your responsibility as a conscious business owner to do your own transformational healing work.

For instance, Jan was working diligently on writing one day and was delighted in the fact that she had overcome her writer's block and gotten engaged in her writing again. After many delays, she was happy to have cleared whatever had been her blockage that kept her from taking the book to the next step. Immersed in her writing, the telephone rang from an acquaintance that she had met briefly who was passing through town and wanted to stop by and say hello. Jan was taken off guard as she heard herself say, "Sure, I'll be in the office all morning, come on by."

She didn't think about the consequence that this woman would be interrupting her train of thought and that she needed to stay focused on the book. The woman arrived in about an hour and as soon as she walked in, Jan could feel the frenzied energy that the woman had brought with her—the last thing that Jan wanted to be around while she was writing! Jan started to notice that the woman spoke loudly and very rapidly about all of her travels and where she was headed without showing interest in Jan or Alan's life. Jan listened to her for a little while and then noticed that her own enthusiasm that she had felt all morning was going downhill. She started to feel tired and the woman just rattled on. Then Jan remembered that the last time this woman had stopped by, she felt the same energy drain from her, yet she had forgotten when the woman called out of the blue.

Luckily the woman hadn't planned to stay too long and left pretty soon after she arrived. After she was gone, Jan noticed she was angry at Alan. (Anger is one of Jan's signals that she has something that needs to be cleared.) Jan was projecting her anger on Alan when she blurted out and said, "That woman drained my energy!

Why did I let her come over?" Then Jan started to breathe and do one of her energy-clearing exercises. Then she called her mentor who helped her to recognize what had happened. The mentor reminded her of another method to clear her energy, which was to wash her face and hands with salt water. She got off the phone and continued to clear her own energy.

Jan learned from her experience and used it to prompt her own self-healing. The woman activated an old unresolved emotion of being lonely and since Jan was feeling the loss of her old friends and wanting to make new friends, she went against her own instincts and allowed the woman to come over spontaneously. Also, Jan was still learning about how to surround herself in protective energy, and she dropped her guard for a moment when she allowed an intrusion in the sacred space of her home from a stranger.

The larger our commitments, the bigger the distractions can be.

Additionally, Jan had just gotten fully engaged into her writing project, which represents a huge commitment that she has and this unexpected intruder helped her to see how easily she can become distracted from her true purpose. The larger our commitments, the bigger the distractions can be.

Fortunately, Jan was able to recognize all of the gifts that this woman provided for her that day and she had a healing, as well as an energy clearing, that allowed her to stay focused on her goal of writing.

If Jan had merely projected her unresolved emotional issues on this woman or onto Alan as if they were to blame for something, then Jan would have never had the opportunity to see what she needed to see for herself.

One other gift that Jan received out of this experience: it showed her how BEE-ing personally responsible gave her power and how projecting blame gave it away to the other person or situation. In every one of the turns and twists of life, you have the choice to go for what empowers you or to choose the victimization that drains your energy.

You may be wondering how to release your own stuck energy and relationship patterns, and what you can do to take on a self-healing process. The first place to begin is by recognizing that you have patterns of attracting. When you have attracted a situation or relationship that is not perfect for you, realize that it is a signal giving you a message. More than likely you will also attract the perfect teachers or healers to assist you in releasing the energetic parts of yourself that hinder your performance. There are many fabulous teachers, healers, body workers, and hundreds of techniques, disciplines, and belief systems to choose from that will assist you. We have had personal experience with and recommend companions to your BEE-ing Attraction Planning process in the Resource Section in the back of the book.

Healing your heart and emotions is part of the work that is required to have what you say you want to attract, and to activate the manifestations that you desire. When you are *not* attracting in accordance with your desires, then it is time to do the work that heals your soul and the BEE-ing Attraction Plan will help surface, and give you access to, healing and releasing what is blocking your true nature from shining bright in the world.

Some of the things you might include on your BEE-ing Attraction Plan about healing and shifting your ability to attract would be added on Part 3 of your plan. For example:

- I am willing to do the healing work that I require to attract the situations and people that prosper me.
- When I am emotionally reactivated, I stop and check to see what inside of me has been activated; then I do the work I require to clear my issues.

- I let all correspondence, verbal or Internet, sit for twenty-four hours before delivery.
- I do my own energetic healing and emotional clearing work.
- I recognize that I attract all situations and use each of them to forward me and my business.
- I keep my heart open and see every person as a reflection of me.

CUSTOMER STORY

The Divine Miss Em
BY EMILY DABNEY

The BEE-ing Attraction Planning Process has had a huge impact on my entire life. I have used the planning process to identify and attract many perfect relationships in my life, including my perfect work life, consulting clients, coaching clients, coaches, attorney, home renovation contractor, whole life, and Self (The Divine Miss Em). I am pretty clear that I am in the process of attracting my perfect husband.

My friend and coach introduced me to the BEE-ing (Strategic) Attraction Process. I was really suffering in my job and she led me through the Strategic Attraction™ Process for my perfect job. Working with the plan made the remaining time with the company much more enjoyable as I had more appreciation for the qualities that did work for me in my current job and as I focused on BEE-ing someone who loves my job and life. My work with the plan also eventually led to the end of that job, as many integral qualities of my perfect job and who I would be BEE-ing in my perfect job and in my life were not being fulfilled.

After the completion of that job, I used the planning process to create my perfect work life. I became clear that what makes me thrive is to do several things to generate income and have a rich, balanced life. I went back to work as an independent consultant in the litigation technology field, where I focus on how I love to be a contribution in that field for my perfect clients.

I do this by consulting with legal teams in using technology to facilitate flow and ease in managing their cases designing custom databases and protocols for each team to utilize the software efficiently and effectively for the way their team works; and teaching and mentoring individuals within the teams to utilize the software to make their work easier throughout the life of the case.

As a personal coach, I use the BEE-ing Attraction Plan with my individual and group clients to custom design, create, and attract whole lives they love and to be their best selves, living their life in alignment with their tick and being the contributions they love to be.

As a jewelry designer, I love custom designing jewelry that captures the essence of my perfect jewelry clients.

As a Nia teacher, I love leading classes in which people really enjoy moving and being self-expressed in and through their bodies. My students report that they feel strong, centered, sexy, supple, playful, and graceful in their bodies, and they take those feelings and ways of BEE-ing out into the world.

As a result of the planning process to identify my perfect work life and my perfect clients, I became clear that my current consulting client was not a perfect client for me, nor was I a perfect independent consultant for her.

Once I completed that relationship, I was hired by my perfect clients and made over and above my financial goal doing only work I love assisting clients who share my values and who honor my tick.

I am paid fees that are in alignment with my skills and work fewer hours, which frees up time for me to focus on other ways I love to be a contribution. If and when my perfect consulting client seems to become less than perfect, I step into who I am to BEE to attract my perfect customer. I have a conversation with the decision makers and redefine our relationship, making it once again perfect. My perfect consulting clients respect my boundaries.

The BEE-ing Attraction Process has made a huge impact on the quality of clients I have, the quality of life I have, and the ease with which both come to me.

During the SACAT Dreamweaver's program this past year, I created a plan for The Divine Miss Em. As a result of BEE-ing The Divine Miss Em, I started living a beautifully balanced, extraordinary life, being my best self and attracting perfect relationships. The women in the Tiara coaching program I participated in this past year acknowledged me for really owning myself, being much more confident and at home within myself, and for knowing what a powerful contribution I am.

I am clear that long-desired and long-awaited goals in my life for which I have created plans are now being realized with velocity and ease, largely because I have finally stepped into BEE-ing The Divine Miss Em. I am now leading and facilitating a coaching group, creating a home environment in which to thrive, and I am in a relationship with a wonderful man.

As The Divine Miss Em, I have easily obtained furniture I love and have easily hired my perfect contractor to remodel and paint my condo to make it beautiful and inviting for myself, my guests, and for my perfect renters. Two years ago I did a Strategic Attraction™ Plan to attract my perfect husband and life partner. In the past month, I have attracted a relationship with a man who seemingly magically fits the plan I created.

When I looked at that plan, I saw that a lot of the Divine Miss Em is on that plan. For the first time in my life, I have experienced the possibility of being deeply loved and deeply loving. If this is not

The Relationship, I am clear it is a huge Sign of Land that The Relationship is on the way. I am clear that identifying what I want, BEE-ing my tick, focusing on creating and BEE-ing who I am called to BEE to attract the perfect relationship daily, and taking actions generated from and in alignment with that BEE-ing, is key to attracting and attaining everything I want.

I am delighted that life often occurs as rich, magical, and easy for my perfect clients and for me!

EMILY DABNEY LOVES WORKING WITH CLIENTS TO CONNECT WITH AND HONOR WHO THEY TRULY ARE, HOW THEY LOVE TO BE A CONTRIBUTION, AND WHAT THEY REALLY WANT IN LIFE. BY PARTICIPATING IN INDIVIDUAL OR GROUP COACHING WITH EMILY, HER CLIENTS HAVE BEEN EMPOWERED TO EXPLORE, DESIGN, AND EMBODY LIVES THEY LOVE, AND TO FROLIC IN THE FLOW OF LIFE. EMILY IS A CERTIFIED STRATEGIC ATTRACTION™ COACH, PERSONAL CO-ACTIVE® COACH, A CERTIFIED NIA TECHNIQUE™ TEACHER, AND PARTICIPATES IN ONGOING TRAINING WITH LANDMARK EDUCATION AND IN THE LAWS OF ATTRACTION. EMILY CAN BE CONTACTED AT EMDABNEY@AOL.COM.

Chapter SIX

Trust, Intuition, and Inner Guidance

"The word psychic comes from the Greek word psyche, meaning 'soul.' Psychic means 'of the soul', therefore, in following the psychic pathway, you are following the pathway of your soul." —SONIA CHOQUETTE, PHD.

How do you make choices in your life? What guideposts are around to help you? How do you get answers that tell you when to move ahead or when to stop? Is there a magic formula, or is there an innate ability that resides within every person?

Trust and intuition play a major part in making choices that you feel good about. If you have trust, then you have a belief that supports your thoughts. Intuition is an innate ability that can be developed by every person when they practice and place *faith* and *trust* in their thoughts. Some call it instinct, psychic, gut feeling, intuition, inner guidance; regardless of what you call it, what we are referring to is the power of recognizing things that are usually not seen by the human eye. These are the things that come through you and are in alignment with your connection to your highest source.

Intuition can help you to grow your business. We could say that intuition is the soil where your seeds of intention are planted. When you think of nurturing your intuition, what are some of the ways to take excellent care of your intuition?

> *"Intuition is a resource that if nurtured, can lead to increased sales, profitable investments, creative inventions, successful hires, advantageous negotiations, bigger profits and increased accuracy in forecasting business trends."* —LYNN ROBINSON

Do you have special intuitive tools that you use? You might be surprised and delighted at how well your intuition is working as a natural ability.

Let's look at three different experiences that you might have had in your life, and identify some of the intuitive tools you may already use. Picture yourself in the following scenarios:

Scene One...

You receive an invitation to a party that sounds fun and exciting. Just before you leave the house, you noticed that the address is one you don't recognize, and so you go to the computer and open MapQuest. MapQuest asks for the beginning address and then your destination, which you enter. In moments, a complete map and written instructions appear, with directions to reach the party and an estimated driving time.

Scene Two...

Now imagine that you have just brought home your brand new car. Installed in your car is a navigational system, called "Genie." You no longer need to print out directions from your computer, because your car can do it all for you. You program into your Genie where you want to go and then Genie does everything except push the accelerator and parallel park. Genie talks to you in a warm, inviting voice. She says, "Turn North on Shepherd," or "Make a left turn on Smith," or "You passed your exit; please exit at the next opportunity." You arrive at your destination.

Scene Three...

You arrive at one of the world's largest shopping malls. Knowing that you are headed for a specific store and not wanting to waste any time searching about aimlessly, you go to the mall directory. You locate where you are, which is denoted by the X— "You Are Here" sign, and then find the location of the store you desire on the map.

These are all scenarios where you have a tool that you can rely on to help you find where you need to go, in an effective, productive, and stress-free way. These tools are great when you have them available to you; however, what do you do when there is no computer, electronics, or maps available to you? Now consider the following new scene, a scene in which there are no clear-cut paths:

Scene Four...

Your former boss, with whom you had a close relationship, contacts you unexpectedly. You worked at his company for many years. He asks you to consider accepting a part-time contract doing the work that you used to do when you were an employee, only at an hourly dollar rate that was twice as high as what you earned in yearly salary. *There is...no "Genie System"...no "MapQuest"...no mall directory.*

All of a sudden your emotions are tied up in knots! Your mind begins to rationalize the offer—you need the money. You were waiting on another contract and it hasn't closed yet. You can see that the money would be really good for now to "tide" you over until the big deal that you really wanted comes through. It doesn't really match your BEE-ing Attraction Plan, however, it is vaguely close to what you said you wanted—*except* for a couple of things.

When you have no tools, how do you choose what is perfect for you? What do you do when you have only yourself to rely on, and you are the only one who can make this choice? Do you take the bird in your hand, or do you stay true to your path? You are torn.

It's time to make a choice, yet where will you go for the best answer that is a match for your current lifestyle, desires, and aspirations? Can you really trust your intuition when you have no idea of what lies in your future? Think of the ways you can use your own inner navigational system to get through the big decisions in your life. Here are some ideas of what others have said about how they would handle making the best choice for themselves. As you read this list, become aware of how you make decisions for yourself:

- *"I go into stillness. I check in with my core. I feel so centered when I check in. I feel whole. When it's not right for me, I feel it in my body."* —MELINDA, LONDON
- *"I become crystal clear about what I want. Good feels good, and bad feels bad."* —ALAN, HOUSTON
- *"I check in with what makes me tick, which is making a difference in someone's life. If what I'm choosing to do is self-serving, then I won't do it."* —JIM, CANADA
- *"I ask for a sign from the universe. I give myself a time limit, and see what shows up."* —PAT, OHIO
- *"I take myself out of my daily distractions, and I look for emotional signals. If there is a tense feeling in my body, emotions like anger that I can't disguise, I will not follow that path."* —JAN, FLORIDA
- *"I decided a long time ago that I will not 'pretzelize' myself to meet a company's needs. If I have to get too twisted up in myself to make something happen, I won't do it."* —NAN, NEW HAMPSHIRE

You innately have the best guidance system money can't buy! One of the most rewarding parts of the BEE-ing Attraction Plan is that it helps you to develop and recognize that you have within you the most supreme guidance system in the Universe. You were born with it.

Think of how babies were born knowing exactly what they need to not only survive, but be happy: milk, rocking, warmth, clean diapers, cuddling, and singing. A baby doesn't have to make a "pros and cons" list when she is hungry or tired. She just knows, and she *communicates clearly* to let everyone else around her know.

There is a highly developed system within you, and when you are making larger decisions in your life (rather than whether you are hungry or tired), you can still rely on these tools. Here are a few of the items that you might pull from your toolkit that can help you make choices: communication, intuition, having a teammate or partner to brainstorm ideas with, listening to our bodies, paying attention, mental telepathy, practicing discernment.

It is very important to trust your intuition and to follow your own guidance system, but you might not have been taking your own best advice. What does it feel like to you when you make a decision that you know you will regret, such as:

- Taking on a client you really don't want to work with or don't like very much.

- Volunteering your time to be on a committee when you have a commitment to spending more time with your family.

- Agreeing to go on an out-of-town business trip when it's your wedding anniversary.

What does that feel like to you? Do you have a feeling in your gut that you've done something wrong? Are you angry all the time? Do you feel guilt or regret? Do you hate waking up in the morning dreading that scenario, and push the snooze button more than normal? What would you do if you had to make a choice that is the best for you, however, others may be angry at you for not understanding your decision?

How about when a decision feels right? What does that feel like to you? Do you wake up in the morning with a grin on your face, excited about the day? Do you call an old friend just to catch up, because you're feeling joy and you want to share it? Do you buy your assistant a bagel and coffee on the way to work? Are you feeling good about yourself inside? Are you more relaxed and feel more confident?

When you are in touch with what you need and what works for you in life, you make decisions that make you happy, and as a result, your energy in life is happy, and does not drag you down. To have total success in BEE-ing Attraction planning is to have total trust in yourself. This is why it is so important to have absolute clarity about what makes you tick and then match your lifestyle, your decisions, and choices to be in congruence with what is most important to you. Once you know who you are and are in touch with this, decisions become a lot easier to make. Just as with a GPS navigation system, when you have a BEE-ing Attraction plan, you know where you are in relation to what is perfect for you.

To have total success in BEE-ing Attraction Planning is to have total trust in yourself.

How do you begin trusting your inner navigational system when you have always relied on your intellect rather than your intuition?

Take for example, Annie, who was living in the small village of Pelayo, Spain. She said that being able to live there is the fulfillment of her fondest dream—teaching the Law of Attraction and sharing her work in a retreat center that she desires to eventually create. Yet moving there after living in the United States and adapting to this major lifestyle change is causing her to pull out all of her navigational instincts and to follow her own intuition without familiar resources to fall back on. Annie writes the following:

"I feel like a shepherdess and literally I sometimes cover ten kilometers or more, by foot, and bus, and mostly it seems so effortless, as I follow my inner guidance...my GPS, until the moment when I realize, my energy has been used up for the day. And then there's usually a day of rest which follows."

We can all relate to what it might feel like to wonder if our intuition is taking us on a joy ride, or if we are in fact, following our designated path.

Sometimes changes in your geography and dramatic changes in your business or life can make you feel like your inner compass is spinning around without any direction. Jan described an experience she had when traveling to a new country:

"When Alan and I were in Italy, we were very much out of our element. We couldn't read the maps since they were in Italian. Our internal directional systems seemed like they were spinning from being in a foreign country, where we couldn't speak the language, plus we were jet-lagged. The first few days were really difficult. We had no connections to anybody in Italy, except to each other. So there we were without all of our usual tools that we rely upon: language, familiarity, friends; what was left was each other, and trust. We had to trust ourselves that we could get to where we needed to go. And soon, as we learned Florence, our hotel became our lighthouse, and we really enjoyed ourselves."

At times you will have to adjust your own GPS by taking the time to do what you need to do. For instance, Emily is a single mother of two. She works out of her house. She gets paid by the hour, so she doesn't want to take time during the day to make her house truly a home. When her kids get home from day care, she is too busy attending to their needs of homework, dinner, laundry, bathtime, and bedtime stories. But every time she is trying to relax or work, tiny things bug her, and attract her negative energy: the bookshelves don't look right, the chair is in the wrong position, and the picture inside the frame is slipping. But what would happen if she allowed herself to take the time, for a few hours each week, to fix her energy-depleting house? It's possible that once she did this, her focus would be much better centered on her goals, her work, and her family.

Perhaps you have heard the quote, "Where attention goes,

energy flows," and in this single mother's case she is also hearing a loud message from her intuition that she needs to take time for herself. The mind can argue with the logic that your intuition is telling you, and many times you disregard the signals that come from your highest source and direct your inner guidance system. You may judge the message instead and add a story about what it would mean if you followed the intuitive side of yourself versus what you think you are expected to be doing. As in this single mother's example, she may also be telling herself that she can't afford to take time for herself, or that there are other things that are more important than taking care of herself.

"Your intuition is your direct pipeline to a form of intelligence that is completely beyond your conscious brain. Successful, effective, happy people are those who have gotten onto the beam of their own intuitive senses and who rely continuously on their inner guidance—and they seldom make mistakes."
—BRIAN TRACY, BEST-SELLING AUTHOR, CONSULTANT, AND SPEAKER

When you are in energetic alignment, you feel good about the decisions that you are making, and when you make decisions that are incongruent for you, it feels a whole different way. Jackie shares an experience where she made a decision and what happened when she made a choice that was *not* in alignment with what is perfect for her:

"I was asked to be a speaker for an event that seemed like a good opportunity at the time. I said yes to be the guest speaker, even though there were no real monetary benefits. In fact, it was something that I would have to drive about twelve hours to get there and pay for my own expenses, food, and lodging, etc. I thought at the time it would be an opportunity to be a in a scenic part of the world, and perhaps it would be a winter mini-vacation. Many things started to feel off for me—numerous inconsistencies with the group I would be speaking to, a bad feeling when I spoke to the coordinating person, and then the weather began to make

driving a hazardous proposition. Three weeks before the event, there were no confirmed reservations for the dinner, and there were no workshop registrations. The book signing that I was going to do had been cancelled because the bookstore went out of business! All of the signs were there, and most important of all I kept having a bad feeling about going. I noticed all of the intuitive signs that this was not going to be a good experience for me, yet I hesitated to take any actions knowing that I didn't want to upset people. I finally called and cancelled my appearance. The person who was arranging the event was furious with me. (Another sign that this was not a perfect match of value.) Nevertheless, I stood strong in the face of someone being mad at me, and took responsibility for stepping over the signals I had received and for not taking action sooner.

In contrast to this experience, I had another speaking engagement happening in the same time frame in which I would also be paying for my own transportation and expenses. In contrast to the first speaking engagement, every interaction that I had with this second group was always enjoyable. I always felt honored and respected. The person coordinating the event was friendly, welcoming, and supportive. I even told her that I had a family situation that could cause me to have to cancel at the last moment and they were very understanding. The two simultaneous speaking events gave me a contrast to see more clearly when something is in alignment with what is perfect for me and when it is not. The challenge is having the courage to say no to what doesn't feel good.

I have always said that when I tell someone "no" that their reaction is an indication about whether I want to do business with them, whether I want to have them as a friend or a perfect customer. In my world, the kind of people that I would call a "perfect" fit for me will always respect my choices and honor my decisions, even if they don't like what I have chosen. When someone gets mad at me for choosing what works best for me, then I know that they are not going to be a good match for me. I have always done my best to give others room to make their own choices and to respect what it is that they have selected—even when it means they tell me no or I tell them no."

JAN H. STRINGER and **ALAN HICKMAN**

Making choices can be opportunities to celebrate, even the chaos of change in your life. Just know that when you make a choice for yourself, then you are doing what is best for everyone around you, even if it makes them angry at first, you still are doing what is the most important thing in every relationship—BEE-ing true to yourself. When faced with choosing, you have the tools to deal with anything and everything that may be involved, and you can feel freedom inside of yourself as you say, "This is fun—this is where I get to choose what is perfect for me!" Enjoy the process of making decisions, and when you choose what's perfect for you, celebrate how that decision helped you to gain the clarity about what you want. That is the essence of your BEE-ing Attraction Plan. It is one more opportunity to step into the BEE-ing of who you truly are by making choices that are in alignment with what is important to you.

Remember—your perfect customers and relationships want what you want!

"One day I went to my computer and looked on the site for some jobs to bid. A job had just been posted for transcription. After reading the description, I realized it was transcribing radio shows on the subject of Law of Attraction. I put in a bid and mentioned that I was currently reading an Abraham-Hicks book and felt very strongly about its teachings. I instantly got the bid (my first). One of the talk shows I transcribed was Jan being interviewed. I felt a connection to Jan. I listened closely to all she had to say. It was quite an experience. At one point Jan said to write a check (for instance payoff of my house) and tape it to my computer. I have done that and I am trying to align myself to receive the opportunity to receive that experience. Really in my heart my true desire is to be a mom! I want to watch my daughter grow. I don't want to miss a second of her sweet life. I am practicing everything I am learning in the book. The person who hired me for the transcription job has really influenced me. She sent me the link to your site. I feel like I am drawing people into my life

now that are like-minded. I am thankful for you and for what you said on that program. I am thankful for the experiences I have been having as a result of opening my mind to the Law of Attraction. I feel warmth when I think of the future ahead of me. My husband and I decided that I should quit my job. I told him I knew that when it was time to pay a bill we will have the money. I have put my faith and focus in the teachings and I know that things are going to work out for me. Thank you for BEE-ing! Thank you for speaking out! Thank you for having a conviction and sharing it with others. Thank you for reading my story." —LISA

Is there anything that you have been putting off in your life? Are there intuitive messages coming to you that you have been ignoring? Where have you lacked the trust in yourself to make a decision or to follow your intuition?

The BEE-ing Attraction planning tool will be your guide for making decisions, as well as learning to trust your gut and follow your intuition in a fun, attractive way. While it also helps you to confront the areas that are "less-than-perfect," it also shows you the way to turn each of these areas around to be in alignment with who you are in this moment. Let go of how it used to be, and take out a piece of paper, and write out your BEE-ing Attraction Plan. It doesn't have to be elaborate or even long, if you have to use a napkin while sitting at a restaurant, do it when you have the thoughts about who you are BEE-ing and who you have to BEE to attract.

Trust that everything that you desire is ready and waiting for you.

Trust that everything that you desire is ready and waiting for you. Imagine that all of the money you want, the treasures you desire, the perfect relationships, the freedom you seek are all waiting for you. Now is the time to withdraw what is yours and create a life that you call **perfect**!

Chapter SEVEN

Signs Guide the Way

"We all have been blessed with a connection that allows the universe to communicate directly with us. To be able to understand the information relayed over that connection, however, it is necessary that we learn to pay attention and know what to look for." —DAILY OM

THE BEE-ing Attraction Plan activates many significant shifts in your business and personal relationships. The changes can be very subtle and overlooked if one is not paying attention. It is one thing to notice the obvious changes, and it is even better if you are aware of each and every sign of change.

The world is full of obvious signs such as street signs, billboards, exits signs, and storefront marquees. But have you ever looked for signs that exist only for you, to point you in the right direction, or show you that you are on the right path? How do you know if something is your sign?

Signs, signs, everywhere the signs are always there pointing the way! A sign is something you notice that grabs your attention. When you notice this sign, you know it is telling you something. Your sign is usually something you find repeatedly, and it seems to follow you around, like finding a feather on the ground or like one of Jan's signs, a carpenter nail on her walking path. A sign that is just for you often times shows itself in a series of three appearances in close time proximity.

> "To see and correctly interpret a sign, you must open your heart and mind to the universe and invite its guidance into your life. Many of us are blind to the signs we receive because we expect angels or our spirit guides to speak to us in a booming voice and tell us exactly what we need to hear. But signs are usually of this earth and therefore easier to encounter. A song lodged in your mind or a number that seems to pop up everywhere you look after you've asked the universe for guidance can both be signs. Signs may come through the animal world, from strangers, or jump out of a book in the form of an insightful passage. A sign may be a direct answer to one of your questions. Other signs may point you in the right direction, warn of impending difficulties, or show you a different way. If you want the universe to send you a sign, tell it that you are ready and willing to accept its guidance. Not everything you hear or see will be a sign. If you are receptive and patient, however, the signs you receive will become easier to recognize. It is important to listen to your intuition. A sign can mean many things to different people, and only you can decipher if a sign's meaning is for you. As you practice reading the signs and following their guidance, the universe will send more of them your way." —DAILY OM

When signs appear, you may be the only one who will even notice it. Why? Because the sign is just for you! It's yours and yours alone. It is up to you to say whether it is a sign or not—chances are, if you are noticing it, and it grabs your attention, then it's a sign.

A sign is something that may also be further represented in one of the following realms:
- Physical
- Emotional
- Mental
- Spiritual

Have some fun and explore your own answers to where signs come from—notice which of the realms are speaking to you and what your inner guidance system is telling you. It might be a message or a confirmation or a warning. Open yourself up to receive and pay close attention to what you are receiving. There is no right or wrong way to interpret your sign, only you get to say what is true for you.

Jan has found carpenter nails for years and never recognized that it was a sign, until one day in a workshop retreat one of the participants said that she had brought a feather, which was one of her signs. All of sudden Jan realized that she had been receiving signs for years and had just laughed whenever she found the nails. She mused that it must be her mission to save people from flat tires. However, after recognizing that these nails were showing themselves to her, Jan began to pay particular attention to them. What did the nail indicate? Was there more for her to understand when she found a nail other than just saving a flat tire?

She began to notice that when she had a thought about something important, often she would immediately notice a nail on the path, which indicated to her that her thought was correct and in alignment with her path. Jan now has a whole collection of these nails—short, long, bent, rusty—and has found them in the oddest places. One particular nail was found on a hiking trail at the top of a mountain after she had been thinking through a whole possibility for one of their programs. Just as she reached a significant realization in her thoughts, she looked down and found a nail at the top of a mountain in Lake Louise, Canada. "How does that happen?" she exclaimed.

Signs appear in threes!

Jan was at the zoo with her young grandson, Slade. As they were leaving the park, Jan looked down the sidewalk and it appeared that there was a zebra standing on the sidewalk. It really grabbed her attention. She pointed the zebra out saying that it looked like it was walking down the sidewalk (the zebra was actually behind a fence), however, it had caught her attention because it seemed to be standing out in the open. That night Jan dreamed about the zebra and just before she woke up, she heard something whispered in her dream state. It said, "If you can manifest a zebra, you can manifest anything you want!" The next day as she was sharing the dream of the previous night to Alan, he then reminded her that there were two other zebras the day before at the zoo. Slade wanted to ride the merry-go-round and after carefully analyzing all of the possible animals to ride, he had chosen the zebra! Then he reminded her that the third zebra was when they went to their favorite restaurant for lunch. At this restaurant they always give the kids a toy with their lunch—and the toy Slade received was—a zebra. Since Jan had seen three zebras in a row and had a dream about them, she realized that there was a message being represented by the zebra. Shortly after that, Jan began to see zebra signs everywhere! It was an amazing synchronicity that all of a sudden zebra fabrics seemed to appear to her in furnishings, clothing, rugs, and decorations. Jan says, "Zebra is my reminder that if I can manifest a zebra, I can manifest anything!"

Signs from the Physical Realm

A sign in the physical realm is something that can be seen or felt in the physical world. A physical sign might also be something that shows up like an ache or pain in your body. It could also be something that is physical to the touch, like a shiny penny, a feather, or like Jan's carpenters nails!

- *"I get a frog in my throat when I'm speaking. It forces me to start listening to the conversation I'm in to hear something very important, or to end the call if I'm not supposed to be involved in it."* —JOE

- *"I feel something in the pit of my stomach, a gripping that tells me to pay attention to what or where I am about to go."* —MONIQUE

Signs from the Emotional Realm

Signs in this realm are described as a feeling. Sometimes the feeling is easy to define such as being happy or sad. An emotional realm sign may be something that you feel in your physical body. For example, you might feel butterflies in your stomach or tightness in your chest. These emotional signs may be something that is felt in your knowing—your inner guidance system signals to you that you are correct or otherwise. You may experience a feeling that is your sign for different messages, such as when you are frightened, or when you have just connected with something exciting. One client burst into tears when she spoke of something that was the truth for herself.

Signs from the Mental Realm

A mental realm sign is something that comes in the form of a thought. These thoughts are different from the zillions of thoughts going through your mind each day—a mental sign is something that stands out like something that you just can't seem to get out of your mind.

This thought is telling you to pay attention to something. By just noticing that you are thinking this thought, you will be able to connect more intimately with the message coming with the thought.

"I simply had to share this story. It made me laugh—perhaps it will cause you to chuckle as well. I had been experiencing some struggle with some teleclasses and workshops that I am offering. I wasn't sure if I was on the right path or not so I asked the universe for a sign. Not wanting to miss or possibly misinterpret my sign, I asked to be shown a rhinoceros if I was on the right path and a walrus if I was on the wrong path. Today I was flipping through a travel magazine that my wife picked up yesterday. I came across a picture of a rhinoceros. I said, "There's my sign," and I offered a prayer of thanks for guidance.

*An hour later I was driving to a meeting. I passed a bus with a large ad on the back for a local restaurant. The name? "The Whistling Walrus!" I broke out laughing so hard I almost cried. I said, "You are messing with my mind!" On the way back from the meeting I saw the same ad again on another bus. And just yesterday I had been joking with a friend that I am very connected spiritually and often get guidance; the only trouble is that it is often in Swahili! So no more jokes about messages I can't understand! Notwithstanding the apparent contradiction, I believe I did get some answers from these signs. Have a wonderful day and may **your** signs be clear and unmistakable."*—DON GIBERSON, SACAT

An example of a mental sign that you may have experienced is getting the name of someone in your head. A few minutes later the phone rings and it's that person you had just thought about. Or perhaps you check for e-mails and find that you have received an e-mail from that person.

Signs from the Spiritual Realm

Some people would say that *all* signs come from Spirit. It is up to you to discern which are your spiritual signs and their messages. Spirit speaks to us in all the realms—so essentially it would seem that Spirit will get our attention one way or another!

Regardless of how you believe or what your spiritual preferences are, each person has a connection to a higher self and you receive signs that send signals to you from that connection. For instance, a couple from California, while visiting friends in another state, was persuaded to look at the real estate market for a possible investment purpose. The husband walked into one of the houses and as he stood in the living room, he heard a message that he recognized as Spirit speaking to him that this was his new home. If that spiritual sign wasn't clear enough, they went back to California and listed their house, which sold within four days. In forty-five days they were living in their new home!

Another client shares this story:

"I hear a very distinct voice. Early on, I was bartending, and deciding how I was going to afford to go back to get my degree in psychology while working. I was at Whole Foods Market, and while I was waiting for somebody to discuss a job there, I saw a brochure in front of me for a massage school. A loud voice went off in my head, and said, "You can do this." Sure enough, I signed up for massage school and pursued my degree in psychology at the same time, and it's led me down a very rewarding path."
–ALAN DAVIDSON, SACAT

Asking for and Receiving Signs

When you ask to receive a sign it is equivalent to opening your arms widely to receive what you desire. The power of asking to receive a sign is about BEE-ing 100 percent responsible for knowing what you want and it signals the Universe to bring it forward.

"I was on a long (twenty-six hours) boring drive but had been listening to spiritual tapes along the way, and one of the points the speaker was making is that God does answer our questions—we just have to listen. I turned off the tape and said, "Okay, God…next town this is it…I want a **clear** sign of whether or not I should go into this sign business with a partner…not just a little sign, but a great big, burning bush with a neon arrow sign…and I want that sign in the next town I come to." Driving into that next town I started keeping my eyes open…and there on the outskirts of town was a huge billboard that simply said, Go for It, (there wasn't even anything being advertised on it—not Nike, not anything—literally that is all the sign said) I kept looking all the way through town and there were about five more "signs" leading me to believe I should go into this business (things that related to it or to my partner, not literally signs). It couldn't have been any clearer. And yet, about ten miles out of town, I started to second guess myself…was that **really** a sign I should do this? Funny how we can second-guess even when the signs are so clear also!

Bottom line, I have now been in the sign business for four years and am living with my partner in the business."
—ADRIENNE LEIGH, MURPHY BUSINESS & FINANCIAL CORPORATION

Many times you want the sign to tell you something about what you want—however, it just doesn't work that way. Play with asking for signs. Remember that all you have to do is ask for it!

"One day I was feeling overwhelmed with a sea of events that were happening in my life. I was resting with my eyes closed and thinking about all of it when I remembered that I hadn't received a sign in quite a long time. As I mentioned in an earlier example, for years I had been finding carpenter's nails—they were always my sign that I was on my path or where I needed to be. In my emotional state, I realized that I hadn't even noticed not receiving a sign until that moment. So I asked to receive a sign that I was on my right path. That same evening, I went for a walk on my neighborhood walking trail. It was dark outside and the street lights offered dim lighting on the path. As I was walking, I was sharing an idea I had for a line of children's books that I had been thinking about writing. I had the idea to co-author the books with my grandsons, Slade and Sloan. Just as I spoke this idea, the light shined enough on my path to highlight a carpenter's nail. It made me stop and I humbly picked up the nail. Tears flowed to my eyes as I realized that I had asked for a sign a little while ago and here was an obvious sign just a couple of hours later. It was that easy!" —JAN

When working with the BEE-ing Attraction Planning process, you get clear what you really want to attract. You specify what is perfect for you in the relationships that support your mission, your vision, your purpose. The reason this key point is so important is that your recognition of the signs along the way gives you an indication that you are in alignment, and your plan is working.

Signs of land are your signals that what you want is on the way! In the book *The Game of Life and How to Play It* Florence Scovel Shinn writes about signs of land. Here is what her book says (you will need to apply your own contemporary language, as her language is from 1925):

"Invariably, before a demonstration, come 'signs of land.' Before Columbus reached America, he saw birds and twigs, which showed him land was near. So it is with a demonstration; but often the student mistakes it for the demonstration itself, and is disappointed. For example: A woman had 'spoken the word' for a set of dishes. Not long afterwards a friend gave her a dish, which was old and cracked. She came to me and said, 'Well, I asked for a set of dishes and all I got was a cracked plate.' I replied, 'the plate was only signs of land. It shows your dishes are coming—look upon it as birds and seaweed,' and not long afterwards the dishes came."

Signs are a way of affirming what you are projecting from your inner desires onto the outer world. It is also a way for the spiritual world to guide you in new ways that may feel foreign or to which you are unaccustomed. You can see that even with all of the modern conveniences in our culture today, like technology or maps, the most reliable system is the one that comes with every person—your human body, mind, and spirit.

"I just got an e-mail from one of my buyers sharing how she wanted some more pieces. She was eager to get the rest of the pieces ordered and wanted to get some more for summer, as the line was doing so well for them! This is a definite sign of land." —SHARON

Your sign is a new dawning of awareness. When you are blazing a new trail in your life, pioneering a new way of BEE-ing, or impacting a major change, you must learn how to navigate in uncharted territory. What is called for is a new dawning of awareness. Signs are very helpful to peak your awareness and will ultimately give you the messages you need to follow.

"I had decided to leave corporate life, and blaze my own career path, but things were slow to start. Because I didn't have to commute downtown, and had no specific time to start my day, I decided to turn off my alarm on my digital clock. The funny thing was that I woke up at the same time, everyday: 7:27. After a week of this, I thought, "What is going on? Is this a sign? What does the sign mean?" And then I realized that the time, 7:27, correlated to my birth date, 7/27. I decided that my waking to the clock at the same time every day was a sign that I was BEE-ing born again in a new life of BEE-ing self-employed, and I considered it a good sign! Whenever I see this numeric sequence it tells me that there is something new is being born." —JAN

What are some of the other signs that you might be seeing that are signs or signals to you? One customer mentioned that her sign comes in the form of lyrics in a song being played on the radio at special times. Another mentioned that she sees a butterfly while another one notices tattoos. This was interesting; a client saw the name "Bruce" used over and over in different places that would catch her attention.

You may begin to notice even more signs every day, and from now on there will be a new dawning of awareness for you when they grab your attention. This is how BEE-ing Attraction tells you that your plan is working—the signs are drawn to you and your energy.

Signs are a way of affirming what you are projecting from your inner desires onto the outer world.

JAN H. STRINGER *and* ALAN HICKMAN

CUSTOMER STORY

What Are Your Road Signs?
BY BETTY HEALEY

Have you ever had the experience of driving a route that you frequently travel, arriving at your destination with little or no memory of how you arrived there? You pull into a parking space and as you unconsciously switch off the ignition key you suddenly wake up. *"Oh my gosh, I'm here! How did I get here? What did I miss along the way?"*

This experience is an apt metaphor for how we navigate the waters of our life. We are often not truly conscious or awake to what is going on around us and as a result, we are not seeing the SIGNS, also called synchronicities, which are showing up every moment of everyday. SIGNS are, in my view, those <u>S</u>ignificant <u>I</u>nsightful <u>G</u>old <u>N</u>uggets that inform your Soul and Spirit. They beg to be paid attention to.

In my experience, paying attention to the SIGNS and consciously choosing the road you wish to travel in life requires two things. First is the willingness to be more present in your life, to be clear about what you want to attract, and to pay attention to the indications that the Universe is responding. This is the practice SIGN Spotting.

Second is BEE-ing authentic; know what makes you tick, who you "BEE"; declare your call to service, what you "do" and know what code you choose to live by, your core values. These three elements are your internal compass, the SIGNS that serve as your guidance system. Embracing your life's journey implies honing your SIGN-seeing abilities, paying attention to what is in your peripheral vision as well as taking the time to reflect on meaning.

SIGNS come in many forms. They may be actual road SIGNS

along local rural routes. They may show up in conversations you overhear which seem to be meant for your ears, stories told to you by a stranger, or on your favorite radio station. A SIGN may be found in a quote or lyrics of a song that registers and won't go away, or a challenge given to you by a friend that puts you on notice. Whatever form SIGNS may take, they are telling you that what you desire to attract is on the way.

SIGNS are personally relevant and may have no meaning to someone standing right next to you. They are the events that show up in your life every day that tickle your intuition. Your inner voice says, "Pay attention to this, it's important."

SIGN Spotting is an essential ingredient for BEE-ing Attractive. SIGNS provide the evidence that you are arriving and becoming the person you choose to be.

BETTY HEALEY, THE ROAD SIGNS COACH, MASTER STRATEGIC ATTRACTION™ COACH, IS THE AUTHOR OF *ROAD SIGNS: TRAVEL TIPS FOR AUTHENTIC LIVING, ROADSIGNS2: TRAVEL TIPS TO HIGHER GROUND,* AND THE SOON TO BE PUBLISHED *ME FIRST: IF I SHOULD WAKE BEFORE I DIE.* YOU CAN LEARN MORE ABOUT BETTY AT WWW.ROADSIGNS.CA.

Chapter EIGHT

Energy Balance and Attraction

"Balance is something to discover moment to moment. You may pile things up thinking these things give you balance. Things are not balance."
—DR. BARRY MORGUELAN

WHEN your energy is in alignment with who you see yourself as BEE-ing in the world, you have a feeling of balance. The feeling of balance can be described as peacefulness, centeredness, BEE-ing "right" with the world. In the ancient Chinese art of achieving balance and harmony in environments, the best chi is located in the most central point of the room or house. When your chi is centered, your body functions better, your house feels better, and you attract easily. The energy or chi that you radiate is in direct proportion to your ability to attract. Ever wondered why a cat may choose to sleep in a particular spot? Cats are sensitive to the best feeling areas of the house, and often times sleep in the center of your house or the room.

You always want to live in a centered place, and love when you feel peaceful inside, and everything seems to be flowing and moving in a positive direction. When you impact a change in your life, a disruption happens before the peacefulness settles in, and it is during these times of change that you desire to have additional tools to support your transition from one place to another.

"The reason that being in energy balance with yourself is so important is that your energy balance equals your point of attraction. You cannot feel 'not enough money' and let more money in. You have to feel it before it can come in! You have to be somewhere in the vibrational range of your desire to even get a whiff of it! What goes wrong with so many, they have a desire vibrating—and they also have a habit vibrating—and then they feel something is wrong because their desire just can't seem to get through. How you feel and what you think about is so important. You have to move your habit of thought closer to your desire. You can't expect one thing and get another. You have to modify some beliefs; you have to change some expectations!"
—ABRAHAM-HICKS WORKSHOP AUDIO RECORDING, MARCH 5, 2005, TRACK 2: THEY HAD PREVOST DOOR ISSUES

Energy Balance Daily Exercise:

If you were going to rate how balanced you are feeling today, where would you rate yourself on a scale between 1 (out of kilter) and 10 (in harmony)? If you are not feeling like a 10, ask yourself: What would it take for me to become a 10? It's also good to know that you can't jump from a 0 to a 10 in one step.

When your life is going smoothly, you may say that you are *in the flow*, or *in the zone*. These are the times when you love openly and it is easy to be excited about life. In contrast, there are times when you have the bumps in the road, life challenges, or unexpected turns.

The best plans can be interrupted by unscheduled relationship shifts, health issues, or money concerns. The important people in your life also impact your ability to balance and can throw you out of sync. How you are affected by these life bumps is up to you, as you have the power to smooth out all the bumps in your road.

Do any of these examples sound familiar to you?

- Things were going so well and then my parent's health crisis took my energy and attention; now I feel drained and tired.
- I have worked so hard to become balanced in my own life, and then my husband lost his job, which caused me to panic.
- The kids have been sick all week and I haven't been able to catch up on my e-mails or open the mail.
- Just when I had started to get ahead financially, my car needed repairs.
- The planning I did all went out the window when my computer crashed, and I just can't seem to get focused again.
- I've been fighting fires all week. I can't seem to get beyond them.

These situations sound like they are out of your control. Perhaps you have lost sleep or can't stop thinking about them. You may have attempted to get your spirits and attitude in the right place; however, your emotions have been running on high. Every business owner can relate to these challenging times and bumps in the road; however, how you come through these times will determine your ability to succeed.

The bumps in the road, if put into a positive perspective, will strengthen your ability to regain your balance of energy. Balance is of key importance to attracting what you will write on your BEE-ing Attraction Plan. There are no easy answers or quick-fix solutions for these times when your energy balance is askew. Many things around may contribute to this imbalance, such as your relationship with yourself and with others, business demands, world situations, your health, the health of your loved ones, financial distress, stress, and many other factors that affect you. This is why learning to balance your energy is so vital to sustaining the outcomes that you desire to attract as denoted on your BEE-ing Attraction Plan.

When your energy shifts it causes a chain reaction. This change is felt by the people around you *and* can determine things like whether customers are BEE-ing attracted to your business, if your money will flow, and how you feel about all of it. In other words, the energy that you are sending out will also affect the people around you in direct proportion to your balance of energy. If your energy is balanced, you may be sending out the signal of peacefulness, centeredness, you are "right" with the world vibrations. If your energy is not balanced you may feel restless, worried, doubtful, bitter, resentful, and angry. You will attract what you are thinking about and how you are feeling about yourself, other people, and situations.

Where are you in this moment?

"Like a lighthouse perched on a rocky shoal, shining a beacon of light to orient ships in the darkness, God's revealing, guiding light shines for me. As I close my eyes in a few moments of silent meditation, I picture myself navigating a boat to my home port. If the waters around me become choppy or I feel that I am in turmoil, I affirm: Peace, be still. Any anxious thought subsides. God's light is illumining my way, guiding me to my safe harbor. Returning to my daily routine, I know that I am one with infinite wisdom. At any time of decisionmaking, I need only turn within to behold God's radiant light. With the way before me revealed, I move forward with clarity and direction." -UNITY CHURCH, *DAILY WORD*

Do a Self-Check test by noticing what you have attracted recently.
  • Have you attracted abundance or lack?

Energy Balance and Attraction

- Are you receiving gratefulness or resentfulness?
- Are you in balance or out-of-balance?
- Does it pertain to every part of your life or only one part?

The BEE-ing Attraction Plan is the perfect way to balance your energy and to shift your current reality. It is the perfect "self-check test" to see who you are BEE-ing and who you choose to BEE to attract your desires. In BEE-ing Attraction there is no situation that cannot be shifted by using the planning process to work through the challenges and life bumps.

It is an easy tool to restore balance and peacefulness in your life, as well as, to turn up your attraction volume.

Three Keys to Maintaining Your Energy Balance

Here are three key areas for maintaining or shifting your energy balance, which are the main benefits of the BEE-ing Attraction planning process. These keys are **Focus, Awareness**, and **BEE-ing**. BEE-ing Attraction restores the ability to feel good about yourself and is a tool to express in writing all that you desire to attract. It is a tool designed to balance your energy.

- **Focus**

If asked, most business owners will say that focus is one of the most difficult things to accomplish in their day. Constantly being bombarded by e-mails, telephone calls, requests and demands on your time can leave the lens foggy rather than that crystal clear vision that we all prefer.

Organizations bring people together for meetings because it helps to focus on a subject as a group. Meetings bring energy and synergy to any subject and helps expand the vision or deepen an understanding. Successful people have discovered that BEE-ing Attraction can sharpen their ability to focus on their business. When groups apply the tool of BEE-ing Attraction to their planning then the velocity to attract is increased tenfold. BEE-ing Attraction is an excellent tool that brings focus to the subject of attracting relationships that we love to be involved with; it also expands our perspective of what is possible and gives us a personal feeling of BEE-ing larger or grander in our own self-confidence.

"The first keynote speaker was Jan Stringer. She asked some of the conference attendees to come on stage. By asking each of them one of the questions of the BEE-ing Attraction Planning process, she showed us how we are able to move forward when we really answer them. It was amazing to see that each of these people became more focused and actually benefit from being with her for about five minutes each! Very exciting! One of her main points that stuck with me was that we should be our own perfect client first—then we'll find our real clients. Our clients are also a mirror of ourselves in a certain moment of our development."
— A POST SHARED BY DAVID KRUEGER, MD

As a result of applying this focus, your perspective becomes clearer and your energy increases because you are more in alignment with your simple truths. You feel better about your life, and this produces more vitality and connection with what is most important to you in the world.

By following the steps to create a BEE-ing Attraction Plan, you are focusing on what is important to you. It helps you to imagine and to visualize, creating a picture of a perfect relationship like painting a picture with words so that you can actually envision the qualities that you want to attract. Additionally, it is about who you have

The art of focusing on what you desire raises your vibration into a higher state that is more attractive.

to become to attract the people to you that will assist you in fulfilling your desires. The art of focusing on what you desire raises your vibration into a higher state that is more attractive. Creating a practice with your BEE-ing Attraction Planning process will strengthen your ability to focus and maintain that state that feels good to you even when all around you is being challenged or rocked. It is a "life bump" prevention program!

• **Awareness**

BEE-ing Attraction calls on the use of awareness that comes from the part of you that tells your guidance system to determine what you would call a "perfect fit." It calls on you to become aware of when a relationship is a perfect fit, when you feel good, when you feel attractive, and when you feel like a million bucks! Energy balance is the result of being aware of what it would *feel* like to have what you say you desire. Doing the practice of BEE-ing Attraction Planning is like asking the Universe to support you in becoming and staying balanced. The planning process creates an energetic muscle building practice that increases with consistent use over time. It taps into your intuitive abilities that increase the more they are exercised.

Eventually you will integrate the energy balance as a way of life rather than a place you strive to be. The process produces awareness of the present moment and draws on your intuitive awareness skills.

Here are a couple of simple ways to build your awareness *and* intuitive muscles:

1. The next time the telephone rings, determine who you think is calling without picking up the receiver and without looking at the caller identification display. As the telephone is ringing, determine whether you think it is important for you to answer the call, or to let it roll over to voice mail.

If you have seen the name of the caller in the display, then determine the reason you think the caller is calling. Then call the person back or answer the call to see if you were on track or not. If you practice this exercise frequently, you will increase your awareness and your intuition will expand.

2. Go on an awareness walk. Practice seeing what grabs your attention and then interpret the significance this item is to you and why you feel it caught your attention.

- **BEE-ing**

BEE-ing Attraction is about "BEE-ing" someone who attracts what you say you desire to have in your life. Many students of the BEE-ing Attraction Planning process have discovered that it wasn't just another "to do" list—it was in fact a "to be" list!

In India, there is a Vedic saying: *yogasthah kuru karmani*. "Established in being first, and then perform action."

"Since creating my first BEE-ing Attraction Plan and participating in your Leadership Intensive and Training programs, my life, career, and my business have been transformed. The Intensive was more than just a learning experience. It was really an experience that changed my BEE-ing. I have recently attracted and bought my first perfect home after years of believing that it wasn't possible. I also attracted my two dream cars including a company car that I don't even pay for. My career has also been transformed. When I signed up for the program, my business was not succeeding, and I was concerned I would have to go back to a full-time job in the industry I had just left. Within two months of signing up for the program, clients started coming out of the woodwork and we experienced a growth rate in our business of just over 266 percent in one year. I also was asked to join the North American Leadership Team for our

company and have since received two promotions in less than six months. There are many factors that have supported me in the past two years, but none has been as critical for me as my becoming a Synchronicity Leader. I'm so grateful for the experiences, coaching, and sharing and life-changing transformation that I received during this program. It helped me see the leadership lighthouse within me that allowed me to create and experience the life I want to have."—DOUG

When you complete a BEE-ing Attraction Plan, the first step to activating your magnetic ability is to step into the "BEE-ing" of your plan. In essence, you are becoming the BEE-ing of your perfect customers, perfect mate, or business partner first, and then taking actions to magnetize these desires to you. Remember, BEE-ing first and from there you take the actions that will be required. Abraham-Hicks (*see page 92*) calls this expectation. Now perhaps the strange name of our planning process makes a little bit more sense to you, as you understand that attraction is about stepping into the BEE-ing of who you have to be to attract what you want. It is about understanding that your energy balance equals your point of attraction, which is your BEE-ing!

"*I was in Costa Rica earlier this year and I met someone who introduced me to PerfectCustomers, Inc. I must say that I find your concept of 'attraction' a unifying concept. It's a framework for everything. It's pulled together all the 'threads' I've been working on. Once upon a time I was pretty fed up with life, now I'm the calmest, happiest, and most successful I've ever been. A personal attraction strategy will enable me to go higher and to help other people go there, too. Isn't it amazing, how a glass of beer and a conversation with a perfect stranger, in a jungle bar can change your life? Now that's what I call attractive.*" —MIKE

CUSTOMER STORY

Good Vibrations: Staying Balanced through the Storm
BY JULIA D. STEGE, MFA/CERTIFIED STRATEGIC ATTRACTION™ COACH

I was blissfully living my life and doing quite well in my business when the news hit. It was so bad and pervasive that I couldn't ignore it. The stock market had crashed and even my soap opera was being pre-empted to let me know about it. I could feel it all over my body; the tension, resistance, and fear were mounting. My husband could feel it too, and he was saying things like, "This is bad, really bad." Even though we were not directly hit by these losses in the market, I began to worry. At one point I even started having visions of *Grapes of Wrath* scenarios and my husband was recommending therapy. That's when I decided to take my focus and energy back into my own hands and get back to my bliss.

I really knew better than to let the external world throw me off balance. I'd been teaching the Law of Attraction Marketing and the Strategic Attraction™ Plan for years, long enough to know that what I focus on expands and that when I feel bad, I'm moving away from what I want. Yes, it would be easier if the daytime television show I TiVo for escape would leave the news out of it. In fact, it would be nice if the world would comply with me more often. But we cannot always control external events; like the weather and the economy, we can only respond to them. It's how we respond to events that determines our experience of life, and it's how good we feel that determines how fast we attract what we desire.

Attention on Appreciation

The news about the economy had lured my attention away from my goals and actual success, and toward an imagined possible future failure. This was making me feel bad, stressed, and vibrationally misaligned. The first step for me then would be to return my focus to what is working in my life. I started an Appreciation Journal and wrote ten or more items in it each night before bed. I thought about my current clients and how much I like them and how they inspire me. I felt how lucky I am to make a living as an artist and to have the freedom to do what I want every day. I wrote about my husband and best friend and our life together in heavenly Sebastopol, California. I remembered my friends both new and old and how they make me laugh and help me to stay on course.

The Vibration of Money

Because part of my paranoia was about possible future financial troubles, I wanted to especially appreciate the money I was attracting. I wrote about how it feels to have money coming in. I remembered and imagined the feeling of going to the bank and depositing checks. I started laughing my way to the bank to make the large deposits and the small ones. I told the tellers that I love depositing money, "It's my favorite thing to do." Knowing that feeling good around money allows more money to flow to me, I took the time to feel appreciation for any income I attracted and take proper care of it.

Similarly, knowing that feeling good about my current clients allows more clients to flow to me, I opened myself to a widened inflow of customers and inquiries, and I began focusing my positive intention on serving my customers even better than before. I paused often to remember how much I love what I do. I spent time each day to center myself and focus on my clients and how I can help them effectively fulfill their missions.

To support my Appreciation Journal and project it out into the future, I updated my Strategic Attraction™ Plan and thought about my perfect customers in-house and those coming to me. I closed my eyes and imagined what my perfect customers are like, what they say, what projects they have for me to work on, how they feel to be around. I imagined myself blissed-out in their presence and then laughing my way to the bank again.

If I noticed any residual feelings of stress because of the news, I knew this would negatively impact my attraction plan, so I set out to take charge of my own vibration.

That Old Familiar Feeling

Perhaps it was the widespread panic promoted by the news media that triggered an old pattern of paranoia in me, but as September waned and October came forth in a fiery blaze, I noticed a vibration of stress and contraction in my body and mind that felt really old and familiar. To clear this old pattern I began taking pauses several times a day with the intention of balancing my physical energy. I brought out my vibration toolkit and experimented with various methods to clear the mind and any blockages in the body.

Daybreak Balancing

I started my day with an hour of meditation and Jin Shin Jitsu[1], a Japanese form of acupressure I learned from a local practitioner. Paying attention to the various pressure points and feeling the blood flowing through my veins helped to focus in the moment, let my thoughts go, and begin my day in balance.

You Are What You Eat

Next I made my morning elixir of wild crafted rainforest herbs[2] and organic nutmilk to fill my body with vital nutrition. I know that I am what I eat, and what goes first into my body must be pure and energetically vibrant. During the day I make sure to feed myself well with organic super foods and maintain physical balance.

My Personal Spa Moment

After spending the morning in front of the computer working on in-house projects and self-marketing, I began to indulge myself in a midday spa moment. Filling the tub with warm water and essential oils[3], I floated for a while and let the waters wash away any lingering stress from the computer. The aroma from the oils helped to bring my focus into the moment and release all thoughts and all resistance, thus allowing what I had attracted to come to me.

It was not unusual to return from these midday retreats to find several voice-mails and e-mails in the in-box with new inquiries and business propositions. I would spend the rest of the day working on projects and then make sure to exercise, eat a great dinner, and have some quality time at home.

What I've noticed as the months have continued rolling along is that when I stay in balance and take responsibility for how I feel, I continue to attract my perfect customers and thrive. My business continues to grow and I really love the people I get to work and associate with every day. I guess you can say I've learned how to "BEE Balanced," and it's working!

[1] More info on Jin Shin Jyutsu at www.healthatyourfingertips.com
[2] More info on Amazon Herbs at www.lifeismagic.com
[3] More info on Essential Oils at www.younglivingoils.com

JULIA D. STEGE, OWNER OF GRAPHICGIRLZ.COM AND LIFEISMAGIC.COM, IS A GRAPHIC AND WEB SITE DESIGNER, A WRITER, A MARKETING CONSULTANT, A RAINFOREST ADVOCATE AND A CERTIFIED STRATEGIC ATTRACTION™ COACH. SHE COMBINES STRATEGIC ATTRACTION™ WITH BEAUTIFUL DESIGNS, ORIGINAL ARTWORK, AND SMART, SUSTAINABLE MARKETING STRATEGIES TO HELP HER CUSTOMERS ATTRACT THEIR PERFECT CUSTOMERS. JULIA'S MISSION TO EXPERIENCE THE MAGIC OF LIFE AND CREATE THE WORLD OF OUR DREAMS IS EXPRESSED THROUGH HER COMMITMENT TO PROMOTING THE MISSIONS AND DREAMS OF OTHERS. SHE IS PARTICIPATING IN THE CREATION OF A NEW PARADIGM FOR MARKETING THAT IS AUTHENTIC, COMES FROM THE HEART, AND ATTRACTS CONSCIOUS ENTREPRENEURS. JULIA INVITES PEOPLE TO CONNECT WITH HER ONLINE THROUGH TWITTER (MAGICALMARKETER), FACEBOOK, LINKEDIN, AND PLAXO, AND ON HER BLOG AT MAGICALMARKETING.BLOGSPOT.COM.

JAN H. STRINGER *and* ALAN HICKMAN

Chapter NINE

You Are Always in the Perfect Place at the Perfect Time

"We can choose to live in harmony with the 13-Moon, 28-Day Calendar of Peace as a universal alternative to the artificial and irregular 12-Month Calendar. In doing so, we are reconnecting with our innate sense of nature's sacred time, that we may find ever-deepening guidance and balance in our relations with the whole of life. Let us reclaim our time as a conscious vehicle for mental and spiritual evolution."
—13 MOON NATURAL TIME CALENDAR

In the Law of Attraction, you will always attract in perfect alignment with where you are in any given moment—there is no other place to be; you can't be anywhere other than where you are right now. This means that you are always in the perfect place at the perfect time—the law of natural time, and the law of attraction manage all of it for you perfectly—all the time!

When you establish BEE-ing, you are radiating in harmony with your positive energy of your thoughts, feelings, and emotions. When something that you want doesn't come to you, it is only because you are not ready to receive the desire—it doesn't mean that you will never receive it—however, you have to be ready to allow, receive, and accept the fulfillment of your desires.

JAN H. STRINGER *and* ALAN HICKMAN

"I started a business shortly after leaving my corporate job. During the first few months after leaving my twenty-year employment in corporate training, I wondered if I would really make it as a business owner or whether I would have to go back to the corporate world to get a job. Then one day a client purchased a package of my products and services. This man then referred another person, and then I added a small start-up company to my client list. In the course of eighteen months, I was regularly attracting new clients to my business. While it seemed slow to me as I began the business, I discovered that I was not ready to have a full client calendar until I had built my confidence in business skills. The ramp-up time it took to build my business gave me the time to learn the skills I needed to be a better entrepreneur." —PATTY

In the Law of Natural Time, there is a time for everything. There are seasons in nature and in life. In the Law of Natural Time, you allow yourself to be in the flow of what is in the present and you know that pushing for a different result will not produce the results you really want to receive. It is as if you are rowing your boat upstream. While it may seem like you are making progress, the natural flow of the river is pushing back against your boat.

One customer, Beth, signed up to participate in several training programs to expand her awareness and add to her business repertoire. She spent months going to the trainings, participating in the teleconference calls, traveling to participate in the classes, and was very involved on a daily basis to integrate the new information. Then one day she realized it was now the perfect time to focus on her own business; her focus shifted and she is teaching a full calendar of students using her own developed material.

The Law of Attraction and the Law of Natural Time manage what is perfect for you. You are where you are and where you are is always perfect. When you want something different than what you are manifesting at the time, then all you have to do is shift your BEE-ing to be a match for the new desires that you want to create.

JAN H. STRINGER and ALAN HICKMAN

When the time is right, you will attract the perfect situation to support your desires. It makes sense that when the Law of Attraction and the Law of Natural Time are on your side, you may notice amazing synchronicities begin coming your way. In other words, you will have more occurrences of strategic synchronicities or "out of the blue" experiences than you could have imagined possible! This is the result of BEE-ing ready, BEE-ing open, and allowing yourself to receive. It is the result of healing parts of you that were preventing you from receiving the desires that you wanted to attract, the people you wanted to be connected to, and the peace that you wanted to have in your heart.

"We met at Century 21 Superstars and I listened to your story with immediate understanding; after twenty years in the business I was starting to think that I needed to be doing this and that, etc. etc. and becoming more and more confused as to why things did not seem to be coming together. I went home that night and went looking for your book because I already knew I had purchased it, because I remembered the peacock on the cover.

I proceeded to begin reading the book and started filling in the blanks and even making a mission statement. It was the second or third evening of my diving into your book and thinking about your lighthouse metaphor, sitting out on my patio, my husband came home from work (all smiles) and said, 'Look what I got today!' By the way, he did not know anything about the concept or the book. Anyway, I look up and he has a lighthouse, about 12 or 15 inches high, that uses solar during the day and lights up at night. He says, 'Isn't this neat, look how this works.' Can you see the look on my face? It still sits out on my patio as a reminder that I only work with perfect customers and they will find me. P.S. I just listed and sold a condo...on the wall as you go into the kitchen there is a picture of a lighthouse."

—JO STAPANENKO, CENTURY 21 SUPERSTARS

Are you a Search Light or a Light House?

Imagine...100 percent of your customers are perfect 100 percent of the time! These perfect people are the ones who you would describe as a perfect fit for you! These perfect people are the ones who value your service, generate substantial profits, and send you referrals on a regular basis.

According to traditional business statistics the 80/20 rule tells us that 20 percent of our customers or clients generate 80 percent of our income. Is that true in your business? What if we told you that the 80/20 rule is not a rule at all—but an old paradigm—a myth. What if we told you there was a simple paradigm shifting system that anyone can use to attract and keep only perfect customers?

Is it possible to attract and keep only perfect customers, people who value your product or service, are a joy to deal with, and make a big contribution to your bottom line?

See how you stand when taking the Lighthouse Test and apply it to your business and personal relationships. After all, business is highly personal.

The Lighthouse Test

Our business is like a lighthouse standing strong and tall on the rocky shore of a beautiful harbor. The water is calm, the sky is blue, and many boats are out at sea. But off in the distance, a storm cloud is forming. It approaches the shore very quickly. The sky is getting darker, the waves are getting rougher, and many of the boats are being tossed about on the water. As the rain and the wind pick up strength, the power of the beam of light emanating from the lighthouse increases. The darker the skies become, the brighter the light shines to provide safety and security in the midst of the storm.

Now imagine that the lighthouse sees that some of the distant boats may not be able to see their light and the lighthouse starts to chase the boats to try and serve them. The lighthouse is frantically attempting to serve all of the boats in the sea. It sprouts legs and runs up and down the beach acting like a search light, doing its best to catch the attention of all the boat captains, attempting to encourage more of them to follow its light.

If this happened, imagine what the result would be!

Most likely, the boats whose captains were depending on a steady, constant stream of light to guide them safely around potential dangers would be damaged or destroyed in the chaos and confusion. Other boats might be steered dangerously close to shore so those onboard could get a better look at the spectacle. Still others would be perfectly content to stay where they are — out at sea, relying on their own navigational equipment.

The result: very few boats would be served well or at all by the lighthouse acting like a search light.

How often are you, your employees, and your co-workers operating like lighthouses standing securely on the shore, attracting and safely guiding the boats (customers) that need your business with your light? How often do you run up and down the beach frantically looking for boats (customers) to serve?

Perfect customers are attracted to you when you are BEE-ing true to your purpose!

So many businesses spend inordinate amounts of time, energy, and money trying to find prospects and turn them into customers. They are like a lighthouse frantically running up and down the beach. Sadly, when they actually get in front of a prospect they often need to bend over backwards to make a sale. They will lower prices, change terms or even alter the product itself. Why? Because it took so much work to actually find someone who was interested in their offering that they just can't afford to let them go and start the laborious process of hunting down a new prospect.

Obviously this is not a great way of growing a business. What you need is a more sophisticated approach, a process of attraction that allows a business to expand from its capacity to serve appropriate, appreciative customers who respond to the company's intent and mission without having to be "sold," "baited," or "snatched away" from the competition.

More specifically, you need to design your products, services, and the business itself with this question in mind: How would I want to be served by this business? This means standing absolutely secure in the knowledge that there are many people who desire exactly what you have to offer. The energy that emanates from such confidence is like the light that shines from a lighthouse.

Lighthouses do not wade out into the water looking for boats to serve. Your responsibility is to stand still and keep shining your own distinctive light, to keep polishing the lens to ensure that your light has the power and brilliance to break through the darkness and attract the attention of only perfect customers. You must choose to only serve customers whose needs are a perfect match for your company and let all the others go.

This is a good example to remember as you are considering whether you are in the place you need to be, or whether you need to change direction when you are not having the results you desire. The lighthouse reminds you of how you can remain who you are even when there is threatening weather and storms all around you. It also helps you to re-establish a strong place to stand when there are a lot of dazzling distractions. The lighthouse metaphor reminds you to remain true to your authentic purpose regardless of the challenges you face.

CUSTOMER STORY

When the Timing Was Perfect for Me
BY MARIAEMMA PELULLO-WILLIS, M.S., LIFE SPARK COACH & STRATEGIC ATTRACTION™ COACH

It was a day in December, just before the New Year. Every year, during those last two weeks in December, I de-clutter, sort, clean up, and get myself ready for a fresh, new start. There on my desk, under one of the piles of "things to look at when you have time," was a CD—an introduction to something called Strategic Attraction™ and *Attracting Perfect Customers*. "Oh, yes," I thought, "I vaguely remember this...I picked it up at a Mark Victor Hansen and Bob Allen event, where I heard Jan speak, about a year ago...it's about time I listen to this..."

And so that day became one of those life-changing days for me, and I began my journey with Jan and Alan and the SACAT team.

After my first teleclass course with Alan, I knew I had to be a certified Strategic Attraction™ Coach. What a *perfect* fit! In my own work, I provide personal blueprints for learning success and life success, and show children and adults how to discover and use their learning styles and personal success styles to go for what they want. I thought the Strategic Attraction™ Plan would be the perfect tool to take this information to the next level—for myself and for my clients. I sensed that this would be a very powerful combination and I turned out to be right!

In my own life the Strategic Attraction™ Plan has made all the difference. It is such an amazing process! First of all, knowing that what makes me tick is "BEE-ing the Spark of Life" has literally changed me inside and out. Everything I think and do now is filtered through my tick. My tick inspires me, empowers me, and directs me. How could I not attract the perfect people and situations for my life if I am BEE-ing the Spark of Life? Not to mention how easy it becomes to come up with logos, slogans, missions statements, promotions, etc., when you really identify with your tick.

My next favorite part of the Strategic Attraction™ Plan is the third part of the plan that asks: *What do I want my perfect customers to expect of me?* This is such a powerful question. It allows me to really go deeply into thinking about how I want to be in all aspects of my

> *When the tick is right, their faces just shine. It's as if they've just fallen in love with who they really are!*

life. If I really want my perfect customers to expect that I allow abundance to flow into my life easily and effortlessly, then I'd better become that person, and I will attract others who also allow abundance to flow easily and effortlessly. If I want my perfect customers to expect that I take evenings and weekends off, then I'd better become that person, and I will attract people who respect and admire me for taking evenings and weekends off.

The Strategic Attraction™ Planning process is so simple and so effective. I've never been so clear about what I want from my work relationships and other relationships. It is so freeing and so empowering!

Besides what it has done for me, I am thrilled that my clients and colleagues have also greatly benefited from this process. I have worked with people individually and in small groups. Helping people to discover their ticks is the most fun and inspiring for me. When the tick is right, their faces just shine. It's as if they've just fallen in love with who they really are!

Through the Strategic Attraction™ Planning process my clients have found the insight and courage to raise their prices, reduce their work hours, begin a new aspect of their business, make time for their interests, let go of relationships, begin relationships, and ask for what they want. One person even realized that she wasn't ready for and didn't want a romantic relationship at this time, even though for the last few years she thought that was what she desired!

Once the Strategic Attraction™ Plan is written out, things start to happen. I made one for my perfect promotion connections, and I have been attracting my perfect promotion connections! An example that comes to mind is the week I was calling various catalog companies to ask if they would be interested in listing my products.

JAN H. STRINGER and **ALAN HICKMAN**

All of a sudden, I got calls from two catalogs that weren't even on my list, stating that they wanted to include my products!

A client made a Strategic Attraction™ Plan for a new business that she had been thinking about for years, and within a month she had her new business and was working full time with her perfect customers! Another client became really clear about what she wanted to attract as she was going through a divorce, and was greatly helped through that ordeal. My favorite story is from a client who was very upset that a new relationship was breaking up, until she realized, "Of course it isn't working, he isn't the perfect partner that I asked for on my Strategic Attraction™ Plan!"

One of my clients summed it up this way: I barely put it down on the paper and it manifests into my life!

I slip sometimes, forgetting to read my plan or neglecting to update it. But here is what I've come to realize: because I have my tick and my Strategic Attraction™ Plan, I will never get off track again! I thought I was clear before about who I am and what I want, but this process has made me so much clearer and continues to make me clearer.

I am determined to live true to what makes me tick, and so that drives all personal and business decisions. If something doesn't fit my tick, I know it's time for changes to be made. In the past I might have had a feeling that I needed to make changes, but I would be unsure and even fearful about what changes to make. Now it is always crystal clear! It might not be totally comfortable to make a particular change (change is often difficult), but I am confident that it is the right decision and can go forward with a calmness and trust that I would not have had in the past. For example, I recently made time to write a book and create several products around the Spark Your Life theme. I couldn't believe how easily it all came about and how much I accomplished in a two-week period!

Knowing my tick and having my Strategic Attraction™ Plan

enables me to more deeply connect with who I really am, give more of who I really am to my customers, and so attract more and more people who resonate with that: my perfect customers!

I will be forever grateful for that day in December when I uncovered that CD and manifested Jan and Alan and SACAT into my life.

MARIAEMMA PELULLO-WILLI IS CO-FOUNDER OF *LEARNINGSUCCESS*™ INSTITUTE AND CO-AUTHOR OF *DISCOVER YOUR CHILD'S LEARNING STYLE, MIDLIFE CRISIS BEGINS IN KINDERGARTEN,* AND *POWER OF YOU NOW!* SEMINARS. AS A LIFE SPARK COACH SHE PROVIDES PERSONAL BLUEPRINTS FOR LEARNING AND LIFE SUCCESS. HER NEWEST BOOK IS *EVER HAD ONE OF THOSE DAYS...WHEN THINGS GO RIGHT!* AVAILABLE FOR WORKSHOPS, KEYNOTES, CONSULTATIONS, WWW.MARIAEMMAWILLIS.COM, M@MARIAEMMAWILLIS.COM

Chapter TEN

The Art of Mastering Space

> *"The proper feng shui of your environment can enhance your environmental qi, which impacts your personal qi. As all of this has an effect on your life force; it therefore enhances the quality of your life. How you use your life force—your attitudes, habits, and ways of being also impacts the quality of your life."* —JUDY MORRIS, FENG SHUI MASTER

IN this chapter, you will learn some aspects of mastering your own space, which is one of the most important parts of BEE-ing Attraction. Space revolves around:

- your environment;
- your physical body;
- your emotional feelings;
- your spirituality;
- your community.

As an entrepreneur you may work out of your home, which involves considerations along with your family space requirements. If your business is in an office building, then you have to blend your space around what is surrounding your office. Space is about your needs such as what you need for personal time. It is also is about how you feel in the space both physically and mentally. Many aspects play into the art of mastering your space and following are some various parts for you to consider.

Creating Your Space in Your Environment

In this example, creating space is about setting the stage of your environment. It's about activating your body, mind, and soul for an activity or in an area where you will be spending time. For instance, if you are teaching a class, coaching a team, or leading a group, it is just as important to create the space for your activity as it is to lead your class. Creating your space takes place before people arrive and once they arrive, your space is inviting to them.

In the Nia Technique, a body, mind, and soul dance workout, students learn the principles of healing arts and martial art movements through dance. Here is how Nia describes creating space in the training manual for teachers:

"In martial arts it is the responsibility of the student to create the space. It is the teacher's responsibility to hold the space. Creating space is consciously using your whole being to prepare the environment. It requires settling into physical, mental, emotional, and spiritual stillness. We define stillness as empty, peaceful listening. To arrive at stillness, sense your being, that part of you that actively rests in the center of all that is. Enter into the center of your physical body. Enter in between your emotions, into the center between love and fear. Enter into the center of spirit. Remain connected to spirit without seeking. Become one by seeking nothing. Quiet your inner dialogue to reach a peaceful state of mind. Rest in the space of mental stillness. As you rest in the emptiness and silence of center, you consciously and actively create space. It is like calmly and consciously setting the table before a feast."

—THE NIA TECHNIQUE©, BLUE BELT MANUAL

The following are examples of how you might create space in your environment:

- Sit in the quiet, still reflection of your environment or physical space to visualize such things as your day, your goals, the people you will interact with, and the goal that you desired.
- Breathe deeply and visualize centering and clearing your energy centers.
- Release any emotions that may interfere such as anxiety, doubt, fear, concern.
- Focus on being grounded and open to allow the natural progression of events to take place.
- Introduce special lighting in the room that feels good to you.
- Light a candle that adds a soft, warm mood.
- Light a special incense that smells good to you.
- Use essential oils on your body that relax you, such as lavender.
- Feel into the energy of the people who will be coming to your meeting.
- Feel into the energy of the people who will be where you are going.

This is an invitation to be present and aware of the current moment in time. Set a goal or intention to create space for learning, for the teacher to be brilliant, for the program to make a difference for you, for the environment to be pleasant, or for the outcome that you desire to attract.

"I take three deep breaths when I'm creating space. The first breath is for balance and energy, the second breath is to bring out the best in me in the moment, and the third is for discovery and letting go of judgment."
—JANET

Space Clearing ToolKit

When Jan first started leading workshops, she had no budget to rent fancy hotel rooms or facilities. She found an affordable room in the Community Center in her neighborhood. The room had nice windows, a kitchen, a beautiful wooden floor, tables and chairs, and only cost twenty-five dollars to use. Many times the room was used for after-school programs and neighborhood board meetings. While the room had the basic needs, there was no ambiance at all. The energy of the kids left a feeling in the room equivalent to walking into a school gymnasium!

Before every one of her workshops that she held at the community center, she spent several hours preparing the space. To create the space, her toolkit included a bag of scarves, a box of candles, smudge sticks, incense, cleaning supplies, and a mop. She cleaned the floor, arranged the tables and chairs to her liking, used the scarves to soften the harshness of the room, and placed a few candles around the room. Finally she lit a sage smudge stick, which is a Native American Indian tradition, where the sage stick is lit, and the smoke is moved around to fill the spaces of the room with the fragrant aroma. Right before the meeting started, she would light sticks of sandalwood incense, which also added an additional aroma and helped the air in the room to become clear of any lingering energy that was left by previous people who used the space.

By placing this much attention and intention to creating the space, when people arrived they were pleasantly greeted by the welcoming environment. Because there was detailed attention given to every part of the space, people felt at ease and so did Jan as the workshop leader.

After the business grew and the size of Jan's workshops increased, she graduated to using hotel rooms. She applied the same techniques to the sterile hotel rooms and was able to transform them into an inviting space.

JAN H. STRINGER *and* ALAN HICKMAN

When she added a new dimension to her business that involved providing in-residence retreats, she carefully chose her retreat centers because she knew how important the environment was to support the kind of transformational programs that she delivered. Because her holistic approach was important, she shopped for retreat centers that had the qualities that was important to her, such as:

- healthy food selections;
- spa services;
- a focus on healing, well-being, and nature;
- ease in making arrangements for the company and for guests;
- interesting terrain for places to walk or hike;
- a meeting room that had space enough for movement;
- special amenities such as hot tubs, swimming pool, or mineral springs.

To Jan, these were vital pieces that made a difference to her in creating space that supports delivering her training programs. They provided comfort as people were going through various changes, processing and integrating the information.

Holding Space

Holding space is a concept that can be interpreted in a micro or macro perspective. In one aspect of holding space, you are like the Nia teacher who is holding space for her dance class. In a broader interpretation, you could be holding space for the world. When you are holding space, you are like the conductor of a symphony who is holding space for the music to occur as they hold their hands up and wave them along with the progress of the music.

Aspects of holding space may include using your thoughts to hold space for another person such as someone who is going through difficult times, you may hold the space for them to be emotional or down in the dumps when you speak with them. You listen to their situation and hold the space for them to move into better times.

> *By creating space for yourself, you can hold the space for others to be magnificent.*

By creating space for yourself, you can hold the space for others to be magnificent. Holding space is allowing others to be in their own process of transformation or change without judging or interrupting their process with your opinions. Holding the space allows others to be greater than they believe they are or seeing them in a way that they might not be able to see for themselves.

You clear your own issues and are there for other people to assist them in clearing their own much like you would hold the hand of a friend who is in the hospital. You don't take on their troubles as your own; however, you hold the space for them to become strong enough to step up to where they desire to be.

Jan holds the space for her training participant's weeks before the start of the training retreat by giving them advice on how to pre-plan appropriately for their training experience. She advises them about how to plan their travel, what to bring, and what to expect during the training time, and even what to plan for after they return home. In essence, she is holding the space for them before, during, and after the retreat by giving them sufficient information.

Another way she holds the space is to invite people to make arrangements with their supporting relationships to let them know that they will not be checking e-mail or phoning home during the training. Again, this is one way to hold the space for people during their training, as well as, supporting the participant to enroll their significant others in holding the space, too.

After a participant arrives at the retreat, people are asked to not leave the retreat center property during the time of the program. This provision is implemented because it holds the space for each person to keep the energy of the group in close proximity to each other. Because the group creates a special energetic bond during their time together, one person leaving the property breaks the special energy that has formed and brings back with them the energy of the outside world. Again, the power is in holding the space individually for you as well as for the group as a whole.

The holding space exercise referred to above is a valuable experience that each person takes home with them as they enter their world after a transformational experience such as a retreat or workshop. Arriving back in the world can be a jolt to the energy system when confronted with a day full of interruptions and distractions.

Once having the understanding of how important it is to hold space, one can implement it with their family, co-workers, communities, and most of all for themselves at anytime. As a parent, many people can understand how important it is to hold space for our children while they are growing and learning about the world. Then it is also understandable that times of personal change, transformation, growth, starting in a new business or job, would require the same quality of holding space for others and ourselves as we would extend to a child.

Another way to hold space is to avoid taking things personally! Practice not taking anything personally when you're in a meeting. Don't make assumptions; find the courage to ask questions and to express what you really want to communicate with others to avoid misunderstandings, sadness, and drama.

> "Be impeccable with your words; speak only what you mean; avoid using words to speak against yourself or to gossip about others."
> —DON MIGUEL RUIZ, *THE FOUR AGREEMENTS*

JAN H. STRINGER *and* ALAN HICKMAN

Holding Space for Others—Especially Your Loved Ones

Jan's daughter is now a fully grown woman, but it's difficult for Jan as her mother not to offer advice. So now Jan has to practice not interfering, and not telling her what is best for her. This is very difficult for parents to do, but if you hold the space in your heart for your child, they can realize and recognize what is important for them. You can be the stillness for another person. You can hold the light for another person. And it is like building a muscle—you have the capacity within yourself to hold space for a lot of people. If people come to you asking for information, you can give it to them because they are requesting it. If you are offering advice, the best advice to give is to trust their intuition and to go back to their BEE-ing Attraction Plan to see what needs to be refined.

The BEE-ing Attraction Plan is the best vessel and framework from which people asking for advice should operate, to find out what makes them tick, and who they desire to BEE in every situation.

Oftentimes you criticize the very people who hold space for you! When Jan opened her company, she hired a very notable business coach (see *Coaches: Carolyn Fine & Associates in Resource section*). This woman primarily worked with Fortune 500 companies and CEOs, and it was a lucky day when she agreed to work with Jan's small start-up of only two people. In their first coaching call, it became apparent to Jan how important it was for another person to help her hold a bigger vision than she was able to hold for herself at that point in time. This coach would hold the space for Jan as she grew into a more confident and successful business owner by keeping her focused on her goals. After the first year, the company was exceeding every sales goal and Jan was holding the space for the company in a much more powerful way. Then one weekend Jan had the opportunity to attend a seminar that was being led by her coach, and as she sat there, she started thinking that this woman was wrong, wrong, wrong. As Jan listened to the woman, she kept critically judging her every move, and after the seminar she stopped using her coaching services. Jan felt she had outgrown her coach and had stepped into the driver's seat.

Months later, Jan was reflecting on the past growth of the business. She realized that if her coach had not been there in the early days to hold the space, more than likely the business would never have gotten off the ground. All of a sudden Jan realized what a fool she had been to so harshly judge and cut off the services of her coach. With a sheepish feeling inside, Jan called her coach to apologize for being such a fool! Fortunately, her coach generously listened to her apology, and let Jan know she was still holding space for her to be great.

When the birds are ready to fly, the mother pushes them out of the nest. Just as Jan experienced with her coach, there comes a time when you have to let go of the people you have been holding the space for and push them out of the nest. It is not uncommon for the bird that is leaving the nest to be angry, or judgmental of the very person that handheld them during their most vulnerable times. Whether you are a business owner, a parent, a coach, a teacher, or a good friend that is holding the space for someone, understand that when your "bird" that has been in your care at some point will naturally want to leave at some point in time. As that person who has been holding space, your job is to gracefully let go of them, yet more than likely you will always hold the space for their success because this is part of who you are for people.

Sacred Space

What does it mean to you to have sacred space? Your answer depends on what is important to you and what you regard as sacred. In many belief systems, there are symbols that represent the sacred such as a cross, Buddha, religious leaders, saints, angels, and many other representations. It is entirely up to you and your viewpoint of what constitutes a sacred space to you. Do you have an altar in your home or office? An altar can be a special place on a tabletop or a corner of a room or a small corner of your desk. Alan lights a candle and incense before every teleconference call he leads as a way to create space that is sacred to him.

In Jan and Alan's backyard, they have created a sacred space outdoors with a flowing fountain, a pond with goldfish and beautiful, flowering plants lovingly arranged with pieces of wood and stone collected from special places they have visited together around the world. Everything is placed with the intention of creating a sacred space of unity, harmony, and balance. Sitting on their patio, they can be in nature and see beauty while hearing the soothing sound of flowing water. Since their office is inside of their home, often they go outside to take a break in their day or to clear their minds of the many details of their business. Having a sacred space in their home gives them both a special place to rest and feel good.

There are places that you might go to that are sacred such as a church, temple, or shrine. Also public parks, gardens, a serene lake, or an ocean can be extremely beautiful places to connect with the part you call sacred and are easily accessible.

Having a sacred space doesn't have to mean going to a place, it can be as simple as closing your eyes in quiet meditation. You have a sacred space inside of you that connects you to your Source.

The key in creating a sacred space lies in setting an intention that can be represented by thought or a symbolic item. For example, if you place a rose in a vase and set it on a table with the intention of bringing beauty to the room, then you will always see beauty in the room. Create your own sacred space in your home or office by placing items that symbolize something of value to you. A sacred space table or alter placed in a special place will help you hold the vision of your intentions.

Creating Sacred Space for Others

In your business, it might be a good idea to have your clients contribute to the creation of sacred space. Sometimes you might pray with your clients, or say an invocation before you start your meeting. Creating sacred space says that you are asking for the support of a higher power in your relationships, which is extremely powerful. This exercise strengthens the purpose of the gathering. Bringing in the divine into your business may be something that you can do as an entrepreneur; however, you may feel that in some businesses it is just not possible. If this is the case, then you can create sacred space in your own way. For example, you can close your eyes and do a quick meditation before entering an appointment, or you can carry a special totem that is in your briefcase or pocket that means something sacred to you; however, is not observed by others.

When you are preparing your BEE-ing Attraction Plan, consider writing what is perfect for you on your plan in these situations. Do you want your customers to pray with you? Do you feel it is important to be able to express your spirituality with clients or not? Is this something wanted to attract more of in your business life?

Sacred space can be created in a way that is a fit for all people—regardless of belief systems!

Here is an exercise that is very easy for all people to understand; it is designed so that it doesn't infringe on anyone's belief systems or doctrines. Jan and Alan use it when people are participating in a training class that is held in person and involves a group that will be sharing the classroom space together. The intention behind the exercise is to invite all of the participants to feel they are part of the space and to feel that they are represented in the room.

A sacred space table is something that is easy to do and everyone seems to love the outcome it provides.

Here is how it works; ask each participant to bring a totem. A totem is simply something that represents what is important to them, such as a picture, a stone, symbol, or anything the person wants to bring to represent them. It can also be humorous, for instance, one person brought an "Easy Button" which says, "That was easy!" when pressed. Everyone always laughed when it was pressed, and it gave the whole group a fun relief at those moments.

The totem is then placed by each person on a table that is purposed with the intention of holding the space for each individual during the program. Additionally, it places an intention, which the participant has on the table to be held for them. Another feature of this ritual is that by placing the totem on the altar, the individual is claiming that they are stakeholders in the program, the space, and the outcome for everyone.

At the end of the program, each person retrieves their totem and the energy that was held is released.

Burning Bowl Ritual

A burning bowl ritual or ceremony is a way to symbolically let go of your past. In the spirit of clearing space, this is one way you are declaring your intention to release what no longer serves you and make room for what will flourish in you most.

For instance, Lisa let go of her disappointment that she had not reached her goal by the end of the year. On New Year's Eve she had a burning bowl ceremony and wrote down her disappointment on a piece of paper. Next she lit a candle and used it to ignite her paper where she had written what she wanted to be released and placed the burning paper in a bowl. Her intention in this exercise was to let go of her disappointment that she held in her heart and energetically in her emotions.

Another client, Shelly, also had a burning bowl ritual for herself. For years, Shelly didn't feel like she needed to worry about whether she was attractive or not, and didn't worry about makeup or hair, clothing styles, etc. And yet, this made her conscious of not BEE-ing or feeling attractive. She conducted business over the telephone instead of working with people in person and out in public so she never needed to show anyone how she really looked. Even so, Shelly didn't feel good about how she looked and that feeling was reflected in her business. Shelly took a trip out to Los Angeles to meet with an image consultant, and worked with her to find a style that she could feel both comfortable and attractive in. Now she feels confident about herself and is ready to present herself to the world. Shelly used the burning bowl to let go of living in chaos, clutter, and unattractiveness, and declared that her future life will be joyfully peaceful while growing in an attractive way. The burning bowl provided a ritual in which she both declared her new intention to present her work in public and released her need to hide at home.

Retreat Yourself!

A retreat is a great way to experience what you want and need in your life. You don't have to wait to attend a public retreat or to sign up for a program just to be able to enjoy a retreat. Here are a few ways you can implement something for you and still reap the same benefits.

For instance, Betsy set aside a week when she won't be working with any clients and she can just concentrate on writing her novel. Her daughters would be away from home on spring break, and she really wanted to take this opportunity to create this amazing space in her office where she can get inspiration from her music, her vision boards, candles, pictures, etc. By planning ahead, she gave herself the time and the focus she longed for to expand her book without any distractions.

Virtual Retreats

Here is another effective retreat idea that can be done via telephone with supportive partners. Perhaps your retreat partner is one person or more than one person that all want to focus on something for a period of a few days or a week. They agree to speak to each other at the same time each day and set their daily intentions together. The intentions may be anything from writing a book, reading a novel, or resting. Each person can also set a sacred space altar with the intention of holding the space during their virtual retreat time. The group can co-create the retreat and add in many of the same things that might be done at an on-site location; even getting a massage can be accomplished locally. The main thing is that people are coming together for a purpose. This is a great way to save the cost of participating out-of-town, and allows you to experience having the same rewarding outcome as a retreat.

What does the importance of creating space, expanding space, holding space, and sacred space mean to you? The answer to this question is a personal exploration that can last a lifetime. In learning about BEE-ing Attraction, you begin to understand the importance of different aspects of space from within you and within your physical environments.

Space in Your Physical, External Environment

Crowded desks, papers left unfiled, and boxes filling a work area do not lend themselves to space. If your work area is cluttered, so too will be your mind. It is very hard to give your full attention to a project when you look around at all the unfinished projects in your space. Spend the extra time to clean up, get organized, and declutter. You will find that your mind functions a lot more clearly on the task at hand.

You spend a lot of time in your home and your office. When you established your home and your office environment, you were all about creating the space to be to your liking; the decorations and furniture were placed to be attractive and yet functional—they pleased you. The physical building is the container that holds your space. It contains memories, creates a mood when entered, and it has a feeling all of its own that reflects the habitants.

Perhaps you have a special area that you consider "sacred space" for meditation, or quiet reflection away from the telephone or television. Whether or not you realize it, you have already experienced creating space, holding space, and setting up sacred space in your primary living areas.

Space in Your Internal Environment

Space in your internal environment is represented in your thoughts, feelings, and emotions. It is an integration of your intellectual understanding and your beliefs. Your internal environment is also represented by organs in your body. Your body is the container that holds the space for you being healthy and is the vehicle for accomplishing your desires in life. Whatever the internal space is, it has a part that we call sacred. It is the part of us that is private and reserved for our deepest connection with our Source, our Maker, with God. The space inside of you is affected by the external environment that you live in, the people, and the places. The degree to which you feel good in your environments has a correlation to all of it.

Sometimes you treat your car better than you treat your physical body. If you have an expensive foreign car, you no doubt know that you have to have regular maintenance and wouldn't consider running it without enough oil in the engine, or subjecting it to driving in rugged terrain or keeping it outside in bad weather. In the same way, your physical body needs to be stored in a good environment, maintained with good "fuel" and proper care, and your internal organs need the right nutrients to function. Good health is the vehicle to reaching all of your goals—so place a large emphasis on creating what you need to have a healthy body, mind, and soul.

Add to your plan any new ideas that you are receiving about space and that you now want to include as an important part of your life.

Your BEE-ing Attraction Plan might include the following:
- will create the space for myself to be healthy through healthy eating and exercise
- desire to have sacred space conversations with my perfect customers
- my perfect customers expect me to set aside time to rest, meditate, and be in stillness daily

CUSTOMER STORY

Stuck in Mexico
—BY WENDY

You want to hear a "perfect synchronicity" story about how I have come to you—listen to this! Due to a roundabout bunch of reasons, I have found myself basically stuck in central Mexico, desiring to return to the United States, but not enough that I'd be willing to leave everything behind and just get on a bus headed north. I am a published, wonderfully talented advertising, editorial, licensing artist, and illustrator who kept attracting lots of decidedly "unperfect clients"—low budgets, taking months and months to pay, and few and far between. Made no sense.

We actually chose to move to Mexico, and after six months we lost our shirts in a real estate deal (why doesn't matter here) and found ourselves minus the forty-five thousand dollars we were counting on. I am a self-employed artist and my husband is a jazz musician so there was no money coming in. After about a year we decided we hated living in Mexico and were living in the biggest pool of scarcity either of us had ever experienced, which seemed so bizarre but the empty cupboards and lack of zeros in the bank seemed to confirm this. We began selling everything we owned: family heirlooms, jewelry, furniture —everything but our studios just to survive.

I finally had the idea that what I needed was a business coach as I had talent, ambition, desire, passion, experience and commitment in spades. I also had a children's book agent, a commercial art agent, a literary agent *and* a licensing agency in the States. So I searched on Google for business coaches, artists' business coaches, and came up with a few names that I was drawn to, one in particular. She and I started e-mailing and there was a real connection. Shortly I realized that this connection was going to cost me more money than I had every month. This business coach informed me she thought that might be the case and she had decided I could defer all payment, until I was "rich and famous," which she felt was imminent. She was so sure of this and so convinced that I would create the business and all I wanted within a short period of time, and then be incredible advertising for her, and her coaching business that she was willing to do this.

Then! The kicker—it turns out she and I had actually met several times twenty years ago and she remembered me and had even felt back then I was going to be incredibly successful. She lives less than ten miles from where I am planning to move back to in the States— and this happened just from me typing into Google on a computer late at night in central Mexico! She sent me your book, which arrived yesterday! So how's that for the Law of Attraction!

Chapter ELEVEN

Planting Seeds of Intention for the Future

"Begin now to forget everything you know or have heard about visioning and planning. Drop your preconceptions and allow yourself to experience what Buddhists call The Beginner's Mind or those on the Christian path might call becoming like a child again."
—JAMIE S. WALTERS, *BIG VISION, SMALL BUSINESS*

From idea to manifestation, BEE-ing Attraction is a planning guide for who you have to *BEE* to reach your fondest dreams. It has been said that vision is 3 percent of the equation in having a dream come true, the other 97 percent is the process of taking each step along the way. However, if the dreamer or visionary never planted their seed of intention in the ground, they would have never seen the end result come true.

For instance, the fruit you may be harvesting today started as a seed that you placed in the ground one day. Every good gardener understands that there are many stages of growth and development to reap a full bounty. Whether your garden is growing flowers, vegetables, a creative project, a business, or a new relationship, every stage is equally important—from idea to manifestation.

JAN H. STRINGER *and* ALAN HICKMAN

When you have a creative idea, you are seeing into your future. Sometimes your ideas are manifested quickly and the results are immediately seen. Some ideas take longer to manifest than other ideas. Consider the following:

Imagine if all of your dreams came true right now!

You would be in a state of shock if everything dropped in your lap at this exact moment.

When the timing is perfect, however, your manifestations seem natural and like the best thing that ever happened to you. So relax and allow your creative ideas to flow to you in their perfect timing.

Remember how it was when you attracted something that you have desired!

One day Jana, who was six years old, filled out a registration slip in her local gift store to win an Easter basket that was filled with candies, dolls, and toys. Later that day, the store owner called to tell her that she had won the five hundred dollar gift basket. Has something like this ever happened to you where there was something you desired and it came to you? Remember feeling like it was a chance happening or a synchronicity? Remember feeling like it happened so suddenly? The truth is that after you become in harmony with what you want, you will manifest your desires. It may feel like things are not happening fast enough or perhaps like nothing is happening at all. Well so does traveling in an airplane—your seat feels static, whereas in reality you are zooming across the sky! However, when that huge aircraft lands on the ground, you realize just how fast you were going. When you raise your awareness about what you desire, your energy builds to higher levels that will ultimately produce at a rate that feels like you are breaking the sound barrier.

The truth is that after you become in harmony with what you want, you will manifest your desires.

JAN H. STRINGER *and* ALAN HICKMAN

Wonder why some ideas take so long to happen?

The reason some ideas take so long to manifest is that you are not ready for them. There is more alignment and harmony that must take place inside of you for your ideas to materialize. When you come into alignment with who you are and what you really want, then you will attract what you desire. When you have prepared a BEE-ing Attraction Plan to attract a particular relationship type and outcome in your business, you attract the perfect people to assist in achieving your desire. These people may be there to assist you in fulfilling your dreams or they may be the answer to what you have requested.

One day Jan was leading a visioning session for a group of people that she coached. Jan began the meeting with a guided visualization that was followed by a period of silence and individual reflection. During the silent meditation, Jan had a grand vision. In that vision she saw that she would be introducing a new technology to the world. Below is a recounting of what she envisioned that day.

"I saw there were a lot of people coming to learn about this new technology. It was something unique and transformative, yet it was something that felt natural inside and was holistic in nature. I saw that the technology had a worldwide audience and was as intriguing to European and Asian countries as it was to North America.

After I opened my eyes from the meditation, I knew that I had received an important message. I was opening to the new idea, yet I had no idea about whether it would ever happen. My mind wanted to know more information and to figure out how to get it done! Immediately my thoughts began to race as I questioned 'how about this?' or 'what about that?'

I shared my vision with the people in the group that were gathering with me that day, and each person agreed to see that vision come true for me as if they were holding something tangible in their hands.

I look back and remember this visioning session; I can now see that my seeds of intentions were being sown for today. I recognize that all of the programs that I have developed over the past few years were important stages of growth that were seeded in that prophetic moment. My first seed of intention for the Strategic Attraction™ and now the BEE-ing Attraction trainings started a long time ago, and the necessary rooting, growing, sprouting, and flowering has produced each reader of this book."

What are the seeds of intention that you are planting for your future?

You can use the art of visualization as a tool that is easy to access at any time of day; it can last for a few moments or can be something that lasts for hours. Even a few moments of visualization can shift your awareness into a different state of BEE-ing. Visualization techniques give your mind a picture of something that is positive and allows you to access your imagination and creativity.

Take a few moments to close your eyes and reflect on the question: "What are the seeds of intention that I am planting for my future?" Begin by closing your eyes and taking a few deep breaths. Sit back in your chair and have both feet planted firmly on the ground. Breathe in through your nose and really fill your lungs. Then blow the air out through your mouth. Again, take a couple more relaxing breaths. Now just continue to breathe on your own and keep your eyes closed.

Allow the visualization to come; do not force it. Engage with your vision quietly and without editing. There may be colors or sounds or words with no images. Let it be just as it is and enjoy your experience. When you are ready to come back into the room, do so slowly by keeping your eyes closed yet feeling your physical body again. Wiggle your fingers and toes. Slowly open your eyes. Immediately without speaking, pick up a pen and begin freely writing or drawing your experience. Again allow yourself to write without editing thoughts from your mind. If possible, share your experience with another person to help bring forth the visualization and ideas.

JAN H. STRINGER *and* ALAN HICKMAN

Have you stopped using your imagination? Have you given up on what dreams you could attract to you and for the world? Did your childlike wonder of play and fun disappear when you became a serious business person or owner? Would you like to have a relationship with people who are a perfect match instead of a good catch? Are you doing what you *love* for a living and *living* with someone who you *love* to share your life with? Is there any area of your life where you have given up?

Remember, don't quit five minutes before the miracle!

Your time is now! When planting seeds of intention and using the BEE-ing Attraction process, the outcome is unpredictable. Often your new-found clarity forces other issues to be resolved that are not in alignment with your newly discovered commitment in life. In other words, the plan is a glimpse of who you desire to BEE, and must match with your lifestyle to feel harmonious and fulfilling.

Maybe you have been attempting to fit in a role that is not perfect for you, or perhaps you are in a relationship that is not a match for who you have become now. Whatever the case may be, you will now have the opportunity to correct the situations that you created when you were experiencing a previous part of yourself. When you have the wisdom of BEE-ing Attraction, you will be able to see more clearly about the steps to take to make the changes required.

It is important to be willing to make changes even if it takes a little work to get there. Be willing to make changes to your life to accommodate the transformations that you are experiencing. Such as, if you have been someone who works day and night without ever stopping, you may need to make a change in your driven work style. Jan has found that she requires taking time to rest so that her physical body has a chance to catch up to all of the other changes that she has implemented into her business and life. Many people have found that daily meditation and/or ten-minute breathing sessions will assist in moving through the changes, calm the mind, and center the body.

It takes two—me and you.

The process of BEE-ing Attraction Planning is intended to be done in partnership with at least one other person. Consider establishing a way to support your growth by working with another person, a buddy, a coach, or partner to share ideas with on a regular basis. While you can work through the planning process on your own, you will never be able to see your own progress unless you are in relationship with someone who can help you to see your growth. Remember that our definition of marketing is building relationships that feel good and are heart-centered. Step out and invite someone to play with you! Using the BEE-ing Attraction plan regularly will encourage you to let your imagination run wild with thoughts and ideas. The plan is about getting creative, having fun, and believing that everything is possible.

It matters less about whether your seeds will bear fruit immediately, and it matters more about whom are you becoming in the process of reaching your targets. Be willing to start small and take baby steps to get your dreams launched. Jan founded the SACAT Corporation at their kitchen table in a seven-hundred square foot bungalow, and now is reaching a worldwide audience.

When you plant a seed of intention, you are stepping into the BEE-ing of who you have to BEE to bring that intention to fruition. Who would you be BEE-ing if you planted a vegetable garden and it produced a beautiful crop of tomatoes, squash, and green beans? You would be BEE-ing a "Top-Notch Gardener" or anything else that you declare about your BEE-ing that inspires you every day while tending your garden.

You are planting seeds that become manifested in your mind's eye to give you a road map for the result that you want to produce in the future—today!

CUSTOMER STORY

Tiara: The Exceptional Women's Coaching Program
BY BETSY SOBIECH

An Example of Planting, Nourishing, Weeding, and Harvesting

The allure of owning my own business came with my master's degree. It wasn't part of the required curriculum, but the graduate program in Organization Development at Loyola included a conversation about starting your own consulting or coaching practice. I was hooked—not only by the idea of starting a business, but also by the possibility of living a creative, fulfilling life. The first seed was planted.

I worked for a midsized consulting firm for two years before I made the leap. Right after completing a huge project, I did it. I started a consulting practice. I quickly established strong partnerships with like-minded (and like-hearted) colleagues, and we created ClearSpace, LLC. During that time we began soaking up all we could find on leveraging the Law of Attraction, and we were lucky to find *Attracting Perfect Customers* early in our process. Strategic Attraction™ Planning became the best marketing practice of ours and a process we shared with our clients. Another seed was planted.

At the core of our consulting practice, we knew early on that we were most passionate about making a difference with our clients. We knew we wanted to support people in accomplishing results while enjoying the process along the way. We were excellent at providing this service for our clients, yet we faced the typical ebbs and flows of running a new business.

In the face of those ups and downs, I would often try to figure out, strategize, plan, and execute to increase our top line and decrease expenses. These are all good business tactics, which all worked to some extent. We would focus our efforts, align on a strategy, and execute at about 75 percent of our desired results time and time again. And I began to lose steam. The excitement of starting a business began to wear off and the uneven cash flow began to wear me down. As the Law of Attraction instructs, when you're beginning to feel down the best course of action is no action until you feel better. I knew it was time to nurture and nourish the seeds that had been planted, instead of trying to force growth.

One of our partnership agreements in our business is that we each participate in growth and development annually. This supports us in nourishing and nurturing ourselves on a consistent basis. At this time, I chose the SACAT certification as part of my growth and development. I wanted to be in integrity in offering the process to our clients while deepening my understanding of the Law of Attraction. It was a reasonable choice with an unreasonable outcome.

It happened on a SACAT retreat. I finally understood the depth and the power of the tick.

In the past, when I approached the question, "What makes you and your customers tick?" I had focused on trying to figure out what makes my customers tick. During the retreat I heard it differently. The starting point is to connect with what makes me tick. That same thing will be most attractive to my perfect customers. This shifted me from my head to my heart. In my heart, what makes me tick is aliveness.

This is when the weeding started in earnest. I learned that once you understand what makes you tick, you must weed anything you are accountable for in your business that is unrelated. You must let your tick be your guide, knowing that whatever you create will be most attractive to your perfect clients. Luckily, I have a business partnership that fully supports me in exemplifying everything we are teaching our clients to practice. So when I came back and let them know that my tick was now running the show, they were completely on board, excited about the possibility.

With my tick in the driver's seat, business planning took on a whole new light. Instead of my mind trying to figure out the next best iteration of our plan, my heart took over. I quickly recognized our seedling women's coaching program as a powerful, unique, replicable program that could be its own division of our business. From this insight, we began to create at a speed and with a sense of ease that had never been present before. Tiara: The Exceptional Women's Coaching Program emerged.

Tiara is a yearlong women's group coaching program designed as an inquiry into who you are, what you want, and how to create the life you desire. The mission of Tiara is to create a world where all women are choosing to lead lives that inspire them. The core elements of the program are acceptance, owning your desires, manifestation, feeling good, purposefulness, and oneness. Tiara is structured so that the same group of women is together for a full year with two Tiara program coaches. The result is a community of like-minded women supporting each other in creating and living a fulfilling life. It's so inspiring to witness what these women create through their participation in the program. We've had babies born, businesses created, weddings, divorces, promotions, and more. Every program is a place for miracles.

In a matter of nine months, we created a detailed five-year business plan, created a board of advisors, branded and launched our program, completed the curriculum, implemented a communications plan, and surpassed our first month's goals. That's the outcome. What's even more amazing, though, is how much fun it is to run this business. That's right—fun and business in the same sentence. I was always proud of starting the consulting practice and the work that we do in that business division. However, jumping 100 percent into my tick and allowing the Tiara program to grow is the most fun I've had and the most effective I've been at producing business results.

Your tick is wise, and I've learned it's the best source of a business, which is a win-win-win for me, for clients, for you financially, and a win for your soul.

BETSY SOBIECH IS COMMITTED TO HELPING PEOPLE LEAD LIVES THAT INSPIRE THEM. SHE IS PART OF THE TEAM THAT CREATED TIARA: THE EXCEPTIONAL WOMEN'S COACHING PROGRAM TO FULFILL ON THAT COMMITMENT SPECIFICALLY FOR WOMEN. SHE IS TRAINED IN PHILOSOPHY, HUMAN BEHAVIOR, CHANGE MANAGEMENT, AND THE LAW OF ATTRACTION. SHE HOLDS A BACHELOR'S DEGREE IN PHILOSOPHY FROM TRUMAN STATE UNIVERSITY, A MASTER'S DEGREE IN ORGANIZATION DEVELOPMENT FROM LOYOLA UNIVERSITY CHICAGO, AND IS A PARTNER IN CLEARSPACE, LLC (WWW.CLEARSPACE.NET). CONTACT HER AT BSOBIECH@TIARACOACHING.COM. LEARN ABOUT TIARA AT WWW.TIARACOACHING.COM.

*Creating Your
BEE-ing Attraction Plan
and Taking Action*

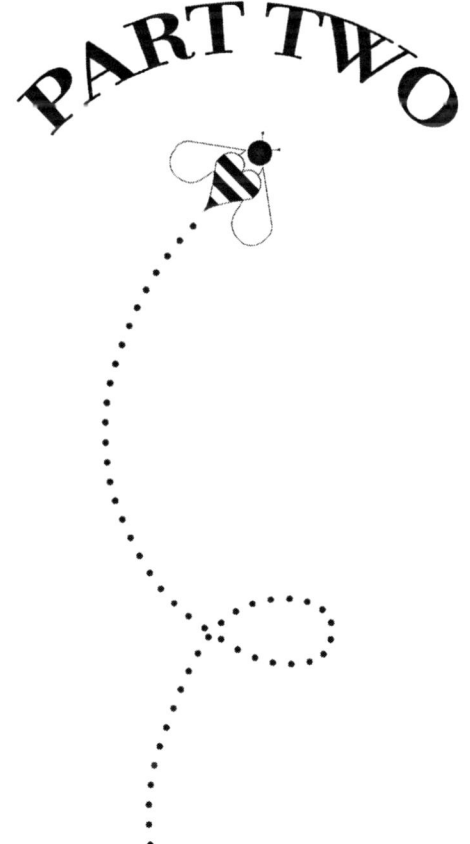

PART TWO

Chapter TWELVE

The BEE-ing Attraction Plan Is About a Deeper Connection With Self

"The life and passion of a person leave an imprint on the ether of a place."
—JOHN O'DONOHUE, *ANAM CARA: A BOOK OF CELTIC WISDOM*

IN this section of the guidebook, you will learn the steps to creating a BEE-ing Attraction Plan for your business and personal relationships. In the step-by-step process, you will be guided to create a working plan. Your plan will change as you do and therefore, the more you reflect your changes and new awareness in the plan, the more it will be alive and fresh.

In this plan, you will describe what is perfect for you in a particular type of relationship, the results that you want to attract in your relationships, and who you get to BEE or become to attract what you say you want in your life. Your plan will also spell out your goals and the actions to take to attract the desired results. It will help you stay focused on attracting relationships and situations that are perfect for you and weed out what is less than perfect for you. Your plan is something that you work on every day by adding new items that are brought to your attention.

"The BEE-ing Attraction Process was first introduced to me through a business coach who mentioned that several of her clients were using it, with great success. The planning process gave me a whole new perspective. I felt my life was in my hands. I could say how I wanted things to go. I was also entering a world of accepting who I am and loving who I am, and trusting that by BEE-ing true to myself, I would attract the people in my life who truly support me. I shifted from scanning the whole field of people, in well-known public places, in search of partnerships and friendships, to BEE-ing comfortable, trusting that I could go where I truly wanted, and I would meet the perfect people. Often when I met someone who was to work with me in some way, our getting acquainted was not even necessary. Somehow we already knew each other." —ANNIE

The act of writing the plan begins a process of awareness and recognizing what may have gone unnoticed or seemed unimportant to you previously. After preparing the plan, you will then begin to work with what you have written in a very conscientious way. Being conscious may involve such activities as meditation, energy, and chakra clearing, and other healing processes that will enhance your ability to attract what you truly desire in your life.

The original Strategic Attraction™ planning process has been shared with thousands of people; it was time to build on what customers have reported as their victories and successes. As you can tell in the customer stories in the previous chapters of the book, they report that they are achieving long-term benefits from the process and people are using the plan again and again.

BEE-ing Attraction takes intention! It takes reaching for your goals. It takes soul searching to discover the areas that are part of you that must be healed. It takes radical personal responsibility to change. The BEE-ing Attraction Plan will have more results if you are willing to follow through with the plan by taking committed actions that are in harmony with your desires. The BEE-ing Attraction Plan will *not* have any results for any length of time until you recognize that everything in your life is a direct result of what is radiating from inside of you, like a beacon to the world.

It requires each person to understand that to attract what you want; you must first heal your wounds so that you can attract new situations that are in perfect harmony with your vision and dreams. The easy part is visualizing what you want; the challenge is accepting your personal responsibility for attracting what you have brought into your life that may be far from the way you want it to be. One benefit of the plan is that you will become aware and awakened that every less-than-perfect situation and relationship that you are attracting is a message from your higher self showing you what is ready to be healed inside of you.

In working with the BEE-ing Attraction Plan, what you write on your plan (especially in the area of romantic relationships) may look more like a wish list or in more cases than not, it is a list that is being written in hope of changing something in your life that is not working or happening the way you want it to. The misconception of the attraction planning process is that often people feel as if they could magically change themselves or another person by writing down something on a piece of paper.

The reality is that the change has to start inside of the person writing the plan first and then others around will begin to shift, too.

Prepare to become energized as you ignite your plan and step into a place of true creation. It is a fun journey and can bring joy even in the darkest of situations.

Jan and Alan got to really walk their talk, as shown in the following personal story of how BEE-ing Attraction Planning can be effective, especially when one is willing to do the work. Here is their story of healing and deepening their connection:

It became apparent to the founders of the process, Jan and Alan, that there was something more that needed to happen in their own lives, which were being reflected back to them by each other and their clientele. They found that they were just like everyone else and needing to go to the next level in their own personal evolution in order to attract and manifest what they wanted beyond what they had achieved. Additionally, they saw a personal challenge being presented to them that needed to be cleared and healed, which had become magnified by a change in their own relationship—marriage. All in all, their issues seemed to be like a sleeping giant who had just awakened and were affecting every part of their life. It was time to follow their inner guidance and what was spelled out on their BEE-ing Attraction Plan. They heard a strong calling for taking committed actions to heal their past and present issues, which were being reflected through their personal and business relationship with each other before they could go any further.

The issues magnified as Jan and Alan discovered that they were gridlocked in a power struggle. The power struggle with each other was causing them to keep attracting less and less of what they desired in their marriage, business, and clientele. It was time for Jan and Alan to begin on a new evolution of understanding about why they kept repeating the same patterns over and over again. While the BEE-ing Attraction Plan was a good tool for sorting out and providing clarity, they needed to break the dance that had formed in their own home and consequently in the business.

Fortunately, they were able to attract the perfect coaches[1] to help them start on the path of discovery where they could deepen their understanding about what was happening with them. Because they were so close to their own situation they saw that they also needed several extra sets of eyes and ears (and a lot of heart!) to help them see what their individual issues were that made them attract the negativity and to start breaking up the old patterns.

JAN H. STRINGER *and* ALAN HICKMAN

They saw how their relationship issues that surfaced in their new marriage were causing many emotional disconnections, which formed long before the two of them came together. Jan and Alan confronted the idea that the energy had become stuck or blocked due to their own individual unresolved emotional issues they had developed throughout their life and with each other. Things that went unhealed in early childhood or wounds that were never healed from previous relationships needed to be opened up to heal and reframed into a new light for them to see how they kept attracting the same patterns over and over again.

Additionally, they had to design a new form of their relationship from being one of primarily a business-oriented partnership to a marriage partnership with the sole purpose of helping each other heal. This was one of the biggest steps in the progress of their understanding and provided a great healing effect, too.

By working with these two gifted coaches[1] in extensive healing, coaching, energy processes, and energetic healing methods, Jan and Alan began to explore the darkest parts of themselves. "Shadow work," they called it, were some of the darkest and brightest moments for Jan and Alan. As the truth became revealed and their energetic blockages were cleared, the healing began.

As Jan and Alan went deeper into themselves and embraced their issues, it seemed that their business of BEE-ing Attraction started to fall apart. At one point they stopped teaching their classes and all of their programs because Jan and Alan knew that something else was being birthed—first inside of them and they hoped one day it would all make sense so that they could resume their business.

During this intensive personal healing period, they were attracted to the energy of another gifted energy healer. Jan and Alan began to work with this energy healer and noticed that much of the beginning work that had started with their coaches was being integrated through the additional work of this energy healer[2] who applied years of dedicated study and practice in Ancient Chinese Energetic[2] healing methods.

JAN H. STRINGER *and* ALAN HICKMAN

They noticed that a new confidence emerged between the two of them and Jan and Alan began to relate to each other in a new way. Now, after their healing had occurred, what they had written on their BEE-ing Attraction Plan started to make sense! Not until they did the work did they see that what had been started as a seed of an idea on their plan was now coming into fruition.

[1] For more information, see Relationship Coaches - Paul and Layne Cutright in the Resource section

[2] See Energy Healing - Dr. Barry Morguelan in the Resource Section

CUSTOMER STORY

Connecting with Who I Really Am
BY ANNIE SHERWOOD

The BEE-ing Attraction Plan is helping me to clarify what is really important to me in a relationship. During the SACAT training, I received one of my most powerful lessons: I am the one responsible for what happens in my life. My life is in my hands, BEE-ing in partnership with the divine energy.

I often review my plan before making a commitment to a relationship, especially a romantic one. I feel free to choose the relationship or not choose it. I feel much better, being patient for the right relationship to begin. In my business, I now understand, why some people are my perfect clients, because we have the same core values. Knowing this saves me a lot of energy. I feel much more peaceful after consistently using the BEE-ing Attraction Plan. It seems the people I am to meet literally show up in front of me.

I have become much more aware of the energy that I hold inside, for I now see how I attract the equivalent energetic vibration. If I experience an undesirable situation in a relationship, I only have to look inside myself to see what is attracting it to me. For example, when I was living in the desert of Morocco, I followed the signs, and I had a long-lived desire to experience the life there. What surprised me is that I attracted two romances, which helped me to see that I had a feeling of being trapped when in a relationship. Literally, in one of these relationships and because of the culture of the area of the world that I was living in, I was told that I was not allowed to leave the house alone. I felt tremendously trapped, and I realized that if I continued to live there I would not be able to continue with my work and my life's passion.

It was then I made arrangements to leave immediately, without having any money at all. I was offered to stay in a friend's apartment if I could make the trip to reach there. What gave me courage was my prior experiences of attracting all of the relationships and resources, while living in Germany and Spain for the prior two years. I never had any financial resources, except for what I attracted along my journey. However, it was a big leap of faith the day I told the driver to take me out to the highway in the middle of the desert, not knowing how I would cross those five hundred kilometers and not having any money or credit cards.

What helps me stay strong is knowing that the divine energy and the divine masters are constantly with me. Out there in the desert, was one of the most powerful testimonies to my own innate power to attract. To accomplish these miracles in partnership with the divine, I had to monitor my BEE-ing. This is a key element in the attraction process at any given moment. I was BEE-ing totally confident and intentional. I was listening to what I "felt" was the next move. There was very little thinking to do, and I had just the minimum of information. It was my attraction plan and a conversation with Jan where I realized that I had attracted this situation to clear out feeling like a trapped woman. It was time to move on.

ANNIE SHERWOOD, SACAT, HOUSTON, TX ANNIESHERWOOD@YAHOO.COM

JAN H. STRINGER *and* ALAN HICKMAN

Chapter THIRTEEN

What Is Perfect for You?

> "Alice was beginning to get very tired of sitting by her sister on the bank and having nothing to do: once or twice she had peeped into the book her sister was reading, but it had no pictures or conversations in it, 'and what is the use of a book,' thought Alice, 'without pictures or conversations?'"
>
> —LEWIS CARROLL, *ALICE'S ADVENTURE IN WONDERLAND*

BEE-ing Attraction is a process to identify and define the elements of your business that you would describe as a perfect fit for you. "Perfect fit" is used in the same way you would select an article of clothing that fits you well, is in your price range, and feels good to wear. In the process of applying the BEE-ing Attraction planning process to your business and personal relationships, you will eventually become in harmony and alignment with your desires. The starting point is to honor your instincts and the ethics that are most important to you, what makes you and your perfect relationships tick, what you want your relationships to expect of you, and who you have to BEE to attract someone, or something, that fits you to a tee.

A BEE-ing Attraction Plan is by no means a quick fix to having your business become 100 percent perfect for you; it is, however, the initial step that starts the ball rolling!

During this discovery process, you will gain clarity about why you are doing what you are doing in your business. This process will help you to understand why some relationships and business opportunities work better than others. Most likely you will be making changes or shifts in many aspects of your business and personal life to accommodate the new alignment that is taking place inside of you as a result of this powerful understanding.

"I have loved the 'That's perfect' wild card, and have tried it out all day yesterday. And it sure does make a difference and has allowed me to trust myself and my Heavenly Father that whatever is happening or going on is just perfect for me and my learning. It's awesome and so freeing!"
—ABUNDANTLY, CYNDI

As you become more aware you will begin to attract more of those qualities. When you are in alignment with what makes you tick, miracles abound! Your energetic vibration is radiating the signal that feels the best to you and this is very attractive.

"I am a United Methodist minister serving a small-town church in rural southwest Virginia. I have read your book (loved it!), worked the exercises, and am applying a Strategic Attraction™ plan for my ministry. I'm excited about the days and weeks ahead and applying your tips to a setting such as a local congregation. I view the customer as the congregant and I'm holding the vision of increasing our worship attendance to one hundred. I identified things I have to improve so that's a plus already. Have a blessed day." —PASTOR JANE

During this transformative process, your relationship to your business will begin to change in direct correlation to your personal changes; some activities that you used to do may even fall away: a long-standing client may choose another vendor, a personal friend may become more distant, or a lover may stop calling you. Just as you might start to worry about the losses, a new idea will emerge that you want to implement into your products and services. When you begin to shift into alignment, a new client might show up that is exactly as you had described on your plan. In the process of change, a new friend is introduced to you who reflects the best parts of who you are becoming, or a possible soul mate appears suddenly. These are the confirmations that show you that your plan is working; you are receiving validation that the changes you have made are being received by the people you most desire to attract.

All of these changes are happening as you personally are shifting, changing, and refining every area of life, business, relationship, and your world. You are consciously creating your business to be a match for what is perfect for you. Now that's attractive.

CUSTOMER STORY

Attracting My Knight in Shining Armor
BY JENNIFER TANGUY (FORMERLY BRUGH)

I'd always dreamed of a knight in shining armor, swooping in on a white horse to take me off into the sunset. What I didn't dream about were the qualities, characteristics, and attributes that he would have. I didn't dream about what would make him tick or about what I wanted him to expect from me.

As a result I jumped onto a few horses and right back off! One day, while riding solo, I came across the BEE-ing Attraction Planning process. This planning process is a simple tool that enlightened me to the fact that if I knew exactly what I wanted in

Mr. Right—I could have it. So I took on the challenge, I feverishly wrote what I wanted—he was 6'1", European, had dark hair, loved to dance, and could dance, was available, loving, etc, etc.

I read the plan I had created every day.

Then *the* day came—Philippe arrived, all 6'1" French inches! I found myself in amazement as I cross-referenced my plan with my "man"—check mark, check mark, check mark. How was this possible? How did I attract Mr. Right so quickly? And then I remembered that by knowing what I want, I am able to attract it.

After dating for a period of time, we just celebrated our six-month wedding anniversary. I wish this for everyone.

JENNIFER TANGUY IS A YOUNG ENTREPRENEUR WHO CURRENTLY DEVOTES HERSELF TO IGNITING PERSONAL AND PROFESSIONAL EXPANSION IN OTHERS THROUGH BRANDING, MARKETING, ADVISING, AND FUNDING EFFORTS. IN PARALLEL SUPPORT OF SELF, JENNIFER IS AN IDEA ARCHITECT SKILLED AT IDENTIFYING A NEED AND DESIGNING A BUSINESS AROUND THE SOLUTION. WWW.JENNIFERBRUGH.COM

"...and all knowledge is vain save when there is work, and all work is empty save when there is love; and when you work with love, you bind yourself, and to one another and to God. And what is it to work with love? It is to weave the cloth with threads drawn from your heart, even as if your beloved were to wear that cloth. It is to build a house with affection even as if your beloved were to dwell in that house. It is to sow seeds with tenderness and reap the harvest with joy even as if your beloved were to eat the fruit. Work is love made visible." —KAHLIL GIBRAN

Chapter FOURTEEN

Creating a BEE-ing Attraction Plan

"What you seek, is seeking you." —RUMI

Now let's get started on your own BEE-ing Attraction Plan!

First, a couple of things to remember—this is a process that evolves over time, so what you get today may be different tomorrow because you will have new insights, new information, and your BEE-ing will be changing along with this process. Also, and most importantly, remember to trust the process! It always works. There have been thousands of people using and experiencing this process successfully who've experienced shifts in as little as ten minutes after working with this concept.

In Part 1 you read about developing a heart-centered business, speaking and sharing from the heart, discovering what truly makes you tick—what you love more than anything. You learned how to BEE, and why you attract the life you have. You've been reminded to trust and use your inner guidance while watching for signs along the way. You also understand now how, when your energy is aligned with what you love, you will attract what you need on the deepest level, at the perfect time, in the perfect place, all while planting seeds for future interactions filled with even more joy, more contentment, more rewards.

Now take what you've learned, and take a deep breath, and try to open your mind to the possibilities, let your imagination run wild as you complete the BEE-ing Attraction Plan. Answer in a way that is true for you, and allow yourself to write whatever comes to you without editing!

There are templates you can use, of the BEE-ing Attraction Plan, on pages 160-163, or simply get a piece of paper and fold it in half to make four sections—two on the front and two on the back.

Your first decision will be to choose what you most want to attract. For example: a client, a coach, a speaking engagement, a radio interview, a tele-class participant, a business partner, a publisher, a coach, an employee, an employer, a perfect mate. Write this at the top of each section:

My Plan *for Attracting a Perfect* _____.

You'll find yourself creating multiple plans to attract many different pieces of a large project, and you'll add pages to update.

Following the templates will explain how to complete a BEE-ing Attraction Plan and show you some sample answers!

THE BEE-ing Attraction PLAN

Overview

My BEE-ing Attraction Plan for Attracting a Perfect _____
(Insert the type of relationship that you are attracting with this plan in blanks.)

PART 1
DESCRIBE the Qualities, Characteristics, and Attributes of your perfect _____.

PART 2
IDENTIFY what makes you and your perfect _____ tick.

PART 3
SPECIFY what you want your perfect _____ to expect of you.

PART 4
DECLARE who you get to BEE to attract what you say you want and give this BEE-ing a title.

Note the first word in each part is a **buzz** word. The buzz words are important to help you distinguish each section of the plan.

THE BEE-ing Attraction PLAN

My Plan *for Attracting a Perfect* _____

PART 1

Describe The Qualities, Characteristics, and Attributes that are a "Perfect Fit" for ME.

Describe what does "perfect for me" look like?

Paint a picture of your ideal relationship. Use lots of adjectives. Think of the traits of people you've already met who are perfect for you, as well as new traits.

How and where will you meet?

Be Specific.

Be Picky.

Keep adding and noticing. What are characteristics of people who are not so perfect for you? Use these to craft a description that is the opposite and more perfect for you.

THE BEE-ing Attraction PLAN

My Plan *for Attracting a Perfect* _____

PART 2

Identify What makes ME and MY perfect customer (or any other relationship) tick?

....
....
....
....
....
....
....

Based on the Law of Attraction, like attracts like, therefore, what makes you tick is also what makes your perfect customer tick. Use the folowing questions to deepen your understanding.

Finally, write down one sentence that combines your answers to all of the following questions:

What do you really love about your life?

What do you want to achieve before you leave this world?

What are you doing when you most love your life and feel that you were meant to be doing this more?

While Part 1 is a long list of qualities and attributes, Part 2 is one statement. Refer to CHAPTER 3 *"What Makes You Tick" to help you answer to this part of the plan.*

THE BEE-ing Attraction PLAN

My Plan *for Attracting a Perfect* _____

PART 3

Specify **What I want MY perfect customer to expect of ME...**

This is the stage of your Plan where you shut the door on sacrifices, and suffering. You get to say... what YOU WANT your Perfect Customer to expect of you.

The clearer you become in what YOU WANT your most perfect customer to expect of you, the easier it will be for them to manifest in your life.

In Part 3, list and consider every detail that is important to you including, and not limited to, how and where you meet, your activities and interests, your availability physically, emotionally, mentally, and spiritually, your financial status, etc.

Remember, your Perfect Customer wants for you what you want. That means getting SPECIFIC about what you REALLY want is the KEY that opens the door between you and your Perfect Customers.

Refer to CHAPTER 15 *and add your goals!*

THE BEE-ing Attraction PLAN

My Plan *for Attracting a Perfect* _____

PART 4

Declare Who you get to BEE to attract what you say you want and give this BEE-ing a title.

_____
_____
_____
_____
_____
_____
_____
_____
_____
_____
_____
_____
_____
_____
_____
_____
_____
_____
_____
_____
_____
_____
_____
_____

In Part 4 you are going to declare your BEE-ing and give yourself (your BEE-ing) a title. In other words, what would be the BEE-ing of someone who accomplishes everything you have said you want in Part 3?

Whatever you have written In Part 3, will happen in direct relationship to who you are BEE-ing.

You must first step into the bee-ing of someone who attracts what you have written; it is a declaration first and then taking actions that draws your desires to you!

Who do I get to BEE to attract what I say I want? And then give this BEE-ing a title.

PART 1

In this section, DESCRIBE the **Qualities**, **Characteristics**, and **Attributes** that are a "Perfect Fit" for you.

This part of the plan is full of adjectives, written as if you were painting a picture of a perfect fit for you. On this part of the plan you will include ideas and thoughts that come into your mind, as well as examples about previous customers and clients who possessed ideal traits. The following questions will prompt your thinking process as you begin describing.

- **What are the positive qualities, the characteristics, attributes, and talents of a customer/client who would be someone you would call a perfect fit for you and your business?**

   For example, you may appreciate the fact that they always say thank you after every transaction. Or, they always return your phone call within twenty-four hours. Or, they place the largest orders of all of your customers. Or, they always have a smile on their face when they greet you. Or, they are always on time for their appointments. Or, they book an appointment every week. Or, they refer other people to your store or web site. Or, they have a sense of humor.

- **How and where will you meet your perfect _____?**

   What would be the perfect way for you to meet your next perfect customer, partner, or companion? Would you like to meet them at a networking function? Or would you prefer to market your business over the Internet? Is receiving your perfect customers from referrals a better fit for you and your business? Consider what is perfect for you and add your answers to Part 1 of your plan. Remember to only add what is perfect for you. Some people prefer Internet marketing and that is perfect for them, while for others they prefer direct mail. To others the best way to meet clients is at a function where they meet face-to-face. What is perfect for you?

- **Remember... in the world of perfect!**

In the world of perfect, you only add what is perfect for you. For example, if you don't like to cold-call or advertise, then don't add it. If you do like using referrals or the Internet, then write that down. The key is to always write items on your plan that are perfect for you in every situation.

- **Add to the list as often as it is perfect for you!**

This part of the plan is a continuing process and you will find that when you place more attention on what is perfect for you, then the more you will attract what you are thinking about and writing down on your plan. It helps to keep adding items on a regular basis—again, you get to decide if it is perfect to add it to your list every day or if you want to do it every week. Your list will grow from just a few words to being several pages long. You may even find that, if you only wrote out this list one time and put it away in a drawer for a period of time, the next time you look at your list, you will see that it has been working for you all the while. Your plan is similar to an artist's canvas on which you are creating your masterpiece.

- **Stay relaxed and alert, this is research.**

Be completely alert to what is and what is *not* perfect for you in every interaction, with every situation, with every person you meet so that you are becoming more aware of what you want to attract. Just as if you were a scientist in a laboratory, consider that you are doing research. Notice qualities in every person that you come into contact with throughout your day, then add those qualities to your list. In addition, watch television, read magazines, listen to the radio—these are all resources for noticing the qualities that you want to have in your life every day. You will find that when your attention is given to what is perfect for you, you will experience more perfect situations rather than what is not perfect for you. The simple exercise of noticing what you want to attract more of draws more situations to you that are perfect for you.

- **Be Specific.**

You already know what you want. Use this writing exercise to record your thoughts and to become more specific in clarifying your desired results. The more specific you are, the quicker your perfect customers/clients will show up at your door and your web site. When you are specific, you are telling the world to serve you in the exact way that you desire to receive your order! Imagine if you boarded an airplane and the pilot came over the loudspeaker to say, "Welcome aboard. Today we have no real destination; we will just see how far this tank of gas will get us!" In essence, when you are not specific, your destination is unclear. By getting more specific details on your plan, you are making a plan that will help you to recognize your perfect customers and clients in the first few moments of meeting them.

- **Be Picky.**

You may wonder if you are being too picky and whether you might be limiting the number of perfect customers you could attract. You can rest assured that the pickier you are, the better your plan will work for you. As a result of being picky you will attract in accordance to your desires. While being picky may have been something that your mother warned you about as a child, in attraction it pays to avoid the pitfalls of working with every client or settling for less than what is perfect for you. In BEE-ing Attraction you end the suffering from all of the times you may have taken less money than was perfect for you or given away too much of your time to get a client to sign or worked with someone who was more of a client from hell than from heaven! So, be picky and end suffering now.

- **No limits here! Just keep noticing and adding.**

What is the perfect number of perfect customers for your business or company to serve over the course of a year? Get outside of your box and write what is exciting. However, also consider if you had the number of clients you listed on your plan, would you still have time for vacations or time to spend with your family, or would you still enjoy your business if your workload had that number of clients? Add the number that would be perfect for you to be working with each day, each month, and each year so that you can be specific and allow time for yourself during certain months of the year. For example, in November, December, and January, will you be taking time off for holidays? In June, July, and August, will you be spending time with your school age children or wanting to take a vacation? Consider all of these factors when you add specifics such as the number of clients you want to work with each year.

THE BEE-ing Attraction PLAN

SAMPLE ANSWERS

PART 1

Describe The Qualities, Characteristics, and Attributes that are a "Perfect Fit" for ME.

They keep their appointments.

They trust that we have their best interests at heart.

They come from a spiritual base.

They already have a growing, thriving business.

They are intelligent and demonstrate good common sense.

They have a strong network of friends and associates to whom they refer us.

They have a financial cushion to pay us.

They pay on time and up-front.

They pay our full fee.

They plan ahead.

They appreciate and take our advice.

They understand and demonstrate that they deserve to be successful.

They know their mission in life.

They make a request to become our client.

They value our time.

They value their time.

They serve the needs of, and make a contributiosn to, the community.

They enjoy paying us.

They provide us with repeat business.

They are peaceful, calm, and kind.

They want us to be successful and make a profit.

They possess and demonstrate mental and physical well-being.

They have offices in great locations around the world.

They have and demonstrate integrity, loyalty, and honesty consistently.

They have realistic expectations of what can be achieved by when.

They want us to work only from 8:30 a.m. - 5:00 p.m. Monday - Thursday.

They are decisive.

They want to personally guarantee their contractual agreement with us.

PART 2

In this section, IDENTIFY what makes you and your perfect customer (or any other relationship) tick.

One pitfall of this part of your plan is that you may be too wordy. Refine it to a simple statement.

For example: *What makes me tick is...working with people to discover a deeper connection to create a heart-centered business.*

The answer to this part of the plan is vital. Refer to Chapter 3 "What Makes You Tick" to help you. Your answer to this part of the plan is short, definitive, and one statement, unlike Part 1, which can be very lengthy and cover several pages; this part of your plan is a simple statement.

In answering this part of the plan, you may find yourself reflecting on the answer for a long time.

Start by asking yourself these questions:
- What gets me up in the morning?
- What am I committed to?
- What is the most important thing in the world to me?
- When I am enjoying my life the most, I am doing *this*; what is *this*?

PART 2

Identify **What makes ME and MY perfect customer (or any other relationship) tick?**

- BEE-ing a catalyst for a new reality in the way businesses operate
- BEE-ing a Legacy Builder
- Shining the light for others to reach their fullest potential
- Connecting people with love and joy
- Making a difference in the world through laughter and lightheartedness

"I would say that one of the greatest gifts I received from being part of the SACAT program and from Jan was my 'tick' (determining what makes me tick). If you look up the meaning of the word 'tick' in the dictionary, you'll find that it means 'to call attention to an item.' It is through Jan's loving attention to the deepest part of us—that self-expression and unique gift that so wants to be revealed from the depth of our soul that Jan has given to me. Our 'tick' is that deepest part of us, our state of bee-ing and how we manifest it in the material world. When it is revealed to us we don't have to 'compete' with the outside world anymore, or worry so much about all the 'doing' because we are clear about our divine purpose and why we were born into this world.

Jan guided me through a process of going deeper into myself so that I could connect with my tick, and most importantly put it into words. Once it came out of my mouth it was as if my life path and everything that I had experienced up to that point made sense. Knowing my tick took a lot of pressure off of me about how I thought it had to look because my Divine expression is a state of BEE-ing. As long as I hold this state then all the other things such as my work, my daily activities, and how I connect with others stays aligned and my life unfolds itself with ease and grace. Thank you, my dear friend, for your wise woman, gentle guidance and precious gift!" —SYLVA DVORAK, PHD WWW.ATMANINTERNATIONAL.COM

JAN H. STRINGER *and* ALAN HICKMAN

PART 3

In this section, **SPECIFY what you want your perfect customer to expect of you.**

This is where you will shift your paradigm—how things are for you right now *becomes* what is perfect for you in your business *by specifying the way you want it to be* in the future.

This part of the plan is useful to see what is perfect for you. Additionally, it is used to change old patterns that no longer work for you, yet you seem to keep attracting again and again; one way to shift an area that is not working perfectly for you is to ask, "What is my complaint? And what would be more perfect for me?"

Use your imagination as if you were drawing a picture of what you want in your business and what it would look like. You can also list anything that you want that isn't happening yet. For example: *I want my perfect customers to expect me to earn one hundred thousand dollars a year or to drive a Lexus or to work with big corporations, etc.* The key is to use your imagination and creativity.

One client added to her plan that she wanted her perfect customers to fly her to an exotic location, all expenses paid, for meetings. A few months later, her favorite client asked her to come and be a guest speaker at one of their annual retreats, which was held on a cruise ship! She exclaimed, "Now that's what I am talking about!"

When something is not happening in your business the way you want it to be, then look underneath the situation to see what is causing you to attract the situation to be the way it is.

In every relationship and every situation, you are the central point of attraction; therefore, you can use Part 3 of the plan to shift your relationships or situation to become a more fulfilling experience to you. This may even be used to promote healing the part of you that is left unresolved, such as what Jan and Alan discovered in their personal healing of past emotional wounds that surfaced after their new marriage.

Here is a great example of how a business owner used this part of the plan to turn a complaint around:

I said, "Tell me what business you are in and what is your complaint?"

She said, "I am a business coach. My complaint is that my clients don't play large enough; they play too small a game and don't take risks in their business."

I asked, "What would be more perfect for you?"

She said, "I would like my perfect customers to play a bigger game."

I said, "Okay, so let's say the opening statement again and apply it to this complaint or situation."

I said, "Specify what you want your perfect customers to expect of you, when, in this case they don't play big enough games."

She said, "I think I just told on myself! Since like attract like, if I am seeing that my customers aren't playing a big enough game, then it must mean that I am not either."

I said, "That's probably correct. Do you play a big enough game?"

She said, "No! I don't!"

I said, "Well then, what would you want your perfect customer to expect of you?"

She said, "I want my perfect customers to expect me to play a big game."

Here are more prompts to help you fill in Part 3

List anything that you would like to happen in your business. Include practical items, such as:
- hours of operation;
- amounts that you would like to be paid;
- the annual sales you would like to produce.

Here you list all the things you want your customers to expect you to have in place, such as:
- to work in an office;
- to work at home;
- to do face-to-face meetings;
- to hold teleclasses;
- to have a web site;
- to have a blog;
- to use social media to market;
- to belong to networking organizations.

Business Operation:
- What are your business operation hours?
- Do you work Monday through Friday, 9 a.m.-5 p.m.? Earlier or later?
- Do you work on weekends? Which days and what time of day?
- What days of the week will you work on your business administration?
- What days will you do client appointments?
- What day will you take time off to rejuvenate yourself or do personal appointments such as massages, nails, haircuts, dental, or doctor appointments?

Sales and Marketing:
- What is your policy around pricing?
- What geographic area will you serve?
- Do you prefer to work from your home or what will be your office location?
- How will you advertise?
- What is the perfect audience for your product and service?
- How and where will your customers find you?
- What products and services are you selling?
- How will you market yourself? Will you be a professional speaker, or will you advertise, or will you do Internet marketing?
- Will you employ a sales staff? An administration staff?
- How much time will you spend on actual selling time?
- How much time will you spend on marketing?

Personal and Professional:
- How will you dress?
- What kind of car will you drive?
- What talents and skills will you become proficient in?
- How many vacations will you take per year?
- How many programs or workshops will you participate in to develop yourself?

As you are approaching the third step, you are moving towards creating a plan that describes what you want to attract in your business and life. Remember—this is where you get to say what **you want** your perfect customers to expect of you. The clearer you become in what **you want** and what you want your perfect customers to expect of you, the easier it will be for them to manifest in your life—quickly and easily. Consider that your perfect customers want what you want. In other words, they want you to be successful and attract everything you say you want. Keep this in mind as you work through this part of the plan.

PART 3

Specify **What I want MY perfect customer to expect of ME...**

- Provide the lowest prices (What does "lowest" mean?)

- Have a business that makes a profit (How much profit?)

- Have a web site for my business (What information would the web site contain?)

- Treat them with courtesy. (What does courtesy look like?)

- Return their phone calls within an acceptable period of time. (What is an acceptable period of time for you?)

- Act professionally. (What does "acting professionally" look like?) Be an expert in my field. (How do experts distinguish themselves from other people?)

- Have a receptionist take messages for me when I am out of the office. (How do you want messages handled when the receptionist is out of the office?)

- Be referred to them by someone they trust. (Would this be a friend, a family member, a co-worker, etc.?) To be available when they need me. (What if they need you at 2:00 p.m. on Saturday afternoon while you are at your daughter's soccer game?)

- Be in communication on a regular basis. (How often is "regular" communication? What do they want you to communicate?)

- To demonstrate radical personal responsibility in every situation and with every relationship, such that when I realize I have been triggered emotionally, I will do my work to clear this energetic block inside of me and never project my issues on to others.

PART 4

In this section you **DECLARE** who you get to BEE to attract what you say you want and you give this BEE-ing a title.

This is the declaration of your intention to BEE what you have written on your plan. Most of the work for this part is already done when you have taken time to be extremely clear and specific in the previous three parts.

Activate your BEE-ing! Read over what you have written on your plan. For example, you might read each item in Part 3 and, for each item, answer this question: Who would I get to BEE to attract what I say I want? Giving a title to your BEE-ing is an exercise in opening your heart and allowing. Your title is intended to be something that you feel inspired by when you declare it and it might even make you laugh out loud. If you or someone who hears your title giggles with delight, then you have made the right choice of titles. The truth always makes us smile or laugh.

In this moment, what is important for you to recognize is that in order to attract you must be ready to BEE the person who attracts this in your life.

PART 4

Declare Who you get to BEE to attract what you say you want and give this BEE-ing a title.

- I am BEE-ing the Goddess through which the impossible becomes possible.
- I am BEE-ing focused and taking attractive actions in alignment with my plan.
- I am BEE-ing the owner of a million dollar business.
- I am BEE-ing a million dollar Hottie!
- I am BEE-ing the Motivation Marketer.
- I am an unstoppable, deliberate attractor of my perfect partners.
- I am the Goddess of insights.

SUMMARY

Your BEE-ing Attraction Plan is designed to **Describe**, **Identify**, **Specify**, and **Declare** who you get to BEE to attract a perfect customer and other business relationships. Additionally, this planning process helps you to understand that to attract you must BEE what you have written on your plan. Lastly, you must take the actions required, which will take you into the direction of what you have written. This planning process helps you to become the person that is in perfect alignment with your true purpose in life and from there you will be developing a heart-centered business!

By virtue of creating this plan, you are making a declaration about a new way of operating in your business relationships and in your life. This is the beginning of stepping into your new BEE-ing and today is the day you declare your intention. The power of declaration and intention will move all of the hurdles in your path!

JAN H. STRINGER *and* ALAN HICKMAN

CUSTOMER STORY

A Spark That Lights Fires
BY WENDY WATKINS, SACAT

Every once in a while, a tool comes your way that supports you on the journey.

For me, it was finding the Strategic Attraction™ Plan. It creates a vehicle that my coaching and training clients could use to integrate the Law of Attraction into their life and build their businesses, and it allowed me to step more fully into my purpose and share my passion!

It all started with a friend who told me about an amazing book that was helping her build her business, *Attracting Perfect Customers: The Power of Strategic Synchronicity*. My curiosity was piqued and I bought the book.

I admit I am not a person who typically works through books step-by-step, but I attracted the perfect partner to work through this book with me. The magic started right away.

I knew that I wanted to build a coaching and training business that was based on my passion and authenticity, which meant not necessarily following the standard rules—actually not following the rules at all! As a result, I fell in love with this methodology. And so the attraction started. New clients, then even more; I knew I had to share this with other entrepreneurs like myself. That is what makes me tick: BEE-ing a spark that lights fires!

This was in late 2005 and early 2006, before the huge success of *The Secret*. As I talked to people about using the Law of Attraction to build their business, I felt like I needed to whisper it softly. In the world of business, the Law of Attraction had not yet become a common concept. My, how times have changed!

After *The Secret*, it was as if a plug had been pulled out of the dam. I had new calls into PassionFruit asking, "Aren't you the company that teaches the Attracting Perfect Customer's class?" Some say that luck is where preparation meets timing; I felt very lucky!

Since then I have had the honor and pleasure of supporting hundreds of entrepreneurs in creating their own unique Strategic Attraction™ Plans.

One of my favorite experiences was with one of the hair salons I work with in Atlanta, Georgia. I introduced the team to the concept of attraction and we created their individual attraction plans, then a plan for the whole salon. That process created an amazing connection to the team's vision and put them all on the same page. The lights went on when they saw that they could provide services that they really wanted to provide, not just services that were expected of them. This has resulted in the expansion of their location and the creation of new, wonderful services and products for their clients. They continue to attract perfect customers and additional team members to support their successful vision.

As consciousness continues to shift, methodologies like this one are going to be instrumental for businesses in attracting more of what is important to them and what raises their joy factor. Overall, that is the biggest impact that I have seen this plan create: it has raised my clients' joy factor. The impact of this, not only on peoples' lives but also on their businesses, is truly amazing. Finding a tool that helps people feel good about marketing is a lifesaver. Most of us know that marketing is about building relationships. This tool creates clarity and power by identifying who to build relationships with and how to do it. When people realize that they can really attract what they want in their own unique way, their joy increases. We all know that when joy increases, we attract much more of what we desire.

Four years later, I am thrilled to report that PassionFruit

Creative People Growers is a thriving coaching and training company. Our foundation is built on authenticity, attraction, joy, and fulfillment. These cornerstones create success for our clients and us. We still use the Strategic Attraction™ Planning process and are evolving as the process evolves. Being a part of the SACAT program as a Strategic Attraction™ Coach honors my value of BEE-ing a lifelong learner, one of the qualities of my own attraction plan!

WENDY WATKINS, PCC, CHIEF GROWER OF PASSIONFRUIT CREATIVE PEOPLE GROWERS, IS A SEASONED BUSINESS LEADER AND COACH WITH OVER EIGHTEEN YEARS EXPERIENCE. WENDY SPECIALIZES IN UNIQUE PROGRAMS AND KEYNOTES THAT HAVE HELPED SCORES OF CREATIVE ENTREPRENEURS IN THE BEAUTY AND WELLNESS INDUSTRY SHIFT THEIR WAY OF THINKING, TAP INTO THEIR PASSIONS, AND CREATE THE LIFE THEY WANT TO LIVE. GO TO WWW.PASSIONFRUITPEOPLE.COM TO LEARN MORE ABOUT WENDY AND THE PASSIONFRUIT PHILOSOPHY.

> *"When I want to stem the flow of clients I stop reading my plan, and when I want to open the valve again, I simply start reading it again! My clients who use it this way to manifest say it works without fail."* —DEANNA RUTHERFORD, THE RAINMAKER

CUSTOMER STORY

Skeptical Me – Out to Prove You Wrong!
BY SUSIE DUKE

After reading your book, *Attracting Perfect Customers*, and because you said I would see immediate results (two days I think), skeptical me was out to prove you wrong and that I couldn't possibly see that kind of results quickly. I did the Strategic Attraction™ Plan and got really into it because I had nothing else to do except sit around since I was on crutches from a cracked tibia and a torn knee. I used my beach house as my attraction center.

Among many of the things I wrote in my plan were:
- I wanted to rent the beach house enough by the end of the year to make ten thousand dollars—unheard of income since I hadn't received that much before, even in the summer (you said ask for the impossible).
- I wanted to rent to families that would come enjoy it and rebuild relationships within their families. Get back to the roots of being a family, eat dinner together, put puzzles together, talk to one another, walk on the beach, and realize who they are again.
- I wanted to rent it for a whole month.
- I wanted people to rent it in advance for the next year.
- I wanted people and families to love my house as much as my family loves the "Chunky Monkey"!
- I wanted to rent it to friends or acquaintances and build long lasting relationships with them.

These were the most measurable outcomes, but in doing the strategy I really got into what I was all about and what was most important to me—family.

I came up with having two family outings with my three children who really hadn't been together in seven years on a vacation.

Amazingly within two days I had four reservations booked for the month of August. In a week I had booked the month between Thanksgiving and Christmas. I accomplished my ten thousand dollars. And the people wanted to rent it the same time the next year.

I rented unbelievably to people I knew through other people on the Internet.

In my guest book, people wrote how much they loved the "Chunky Monkey" and how it had brought their families closer.

I became a believer of your strategies.

The best part is after I got off my crutches, my three kids and I took two different weekend trips together to rebuild all the relationships that had fallen with my divorce. It was incredible. I just want to thank you for writing your book and continuing to promote your strategy. I need to go work on my next plan.

SUSIE DUKE, WWW.INVESTMENTADVISORSINTERNATIONAL.COM

Chapter FIFTEEN

Setting Goals in the Energy of BEE-ing

"Energy is the essence of life. Every day you decide how you are going to use it by knowing what you want and what it takes to reach that goal, and by maintaining focus." —OPRAH WINFREY

AFTER you have created your BEE-ing Attraction Plan, it is time to get into action.

Your BEE-ing combined with action will set into motion your ability to attract. In other words, if you take no actions then your chances of attracting what you say you want are drastically reduced, and it is possible you may not attract anything at all. In this chapter, you will learn a new way to combine your goals with your BEE-ing, which will inspire you and makes your daily actions more enjoyable—less struggle, less feeling of hard work. You will feel the reward of your efforts in terms of achievement and success as well as inner fulfillment.

To set your goals, the same principles apply as on your BEE-ing Attraction Plan. By starting with your BEE-ing Attraction Plan first, you are getting a good idea of what you want, who you want to attract, and who you get to BEE every day to attract it. Additionally, by identifying what makes you tick you are in tune with what is most important to you in life and you will want this to be reflected in your business goals and actions. Clarity, focus, and a deeper understanding apply to setting your goals as well.

"I've gotten a lot clearer on what I want, and the refinement of my BEE-ing Attraction Plan has helped me to get specific about my money and client goals. I hadn't actually written them down! They are now part of my plan." —PHIL

Your plan has given you a deeper understanding of yourself, and from this place your business will begin to align itself with you. You may have experienced the effect of your business before you chose to be in alignment with your purpose and what is important to you; if so you probably noticed that you were not as happy, fulfilled, or satisfied as you would like to be and perhaps you felt burned out after a period of time. No longer sustained by the adrenalin rush of BEE-ing everything to everyone, you became attracted to this body of understanding and were drawn to learn how to align your business goals to become a match for your inner goals. In essence, you made a conscious decision to align your business goals with your soul and commit to BEE-ing on the path of developing your heart-centered business.

"Just writing my goals for the day and taking action daily helps me get to the larger goals without getting overwhelmed." —SHARON

Why allowing rather than achieving?

Setting goals is nothing new. After all, you weren't born yesterday; you were taught to set a goal from the time you learned to walk. As you went through your early years of school and training, goals were set and achieved. School is over now—you are not here to learn anything new. You are here to turn the skills you already have into ones that might become more fruitful or perhaps bring you new successes. If you desire to have success with the goals that you have been dreaming of and still not manifested yet, then you might be reading this wanting to learn something new. Allowing is the way, achieving is the old method of doing business. The good news is that it is time to stop working to achieve and time to start allowing yourself the rewards now. The one thing that will bring you real success in manifestation is when you first **allow** it to happen.

What would it look like to allow?

- Allowing looks like giving yourself permission to have the outcome you desire before the goal is completed.
- Allowing looks like being able to activate all of your senses of the goal being fulfilled, such as to see, smell, feel, touch, resonate, align, and actually BEE the goal before it has happened.

Tiger Woods' dad asked him when he was just a young boy starting to play golf how he hit the hole so easily, to which Tiger Woods replied, "I just see it first Daddy, and then I hit the ball."

Not knowing is a plus!

You might be feeling that you are unsure of your goals. That's okay to not know! In fact, you might consider it a plus or a positive place because you can be truly creative and anything is possible. Use this chapter to help you to formulate your specific goals and begin to focus on the results that you want to achieve.

It's about flowing in rather than pushing out.

While learning this method of setting and achieving goals, it will be an opportunity to let the ideas start to flow in rather than push them out. The intention is to go with the flow of the Universe and to be in perfect time. There will be plenty of time ahead for getting the energy that will have your goals become successful.

In the Law of Natural Time, everything has a time and place. Time is relative to getting your goals accomplished; sometimes there is a delay in receiving the results. By taking consistent actions towards your goals, you will eventually receive what you want to attract or something better will come your way. Often the results of your actions will steer you into a different direction completely, however, that is part of the process. Trust the process and allow things to come to you naturally.

Trust your intuitive sense of your goals.

When setting your goals always listen to your intuitive sense before taking actions. Your intuitive sense is also known as your "gut feeling" as discussed in the previous chapter. For example, if you started to write down a goal but you hesitated before writing it down, ask yourself why you hesitated. If you have a goal that you have written down, yet discover that you cannot get motivated to move forward, then this is not the right goal for you. Your intuition is telling you to go in a different direction or that this goal is not in alignment with your purpose or path. Learn to trust your intuition, which is always going to guide you to what is right for you.

Tell the truth and be honest with yourself.

It is important to be honest with yourself and others about your goals. If you lie to yourself about a goal, your results will be minimal, if any. Other people will be misled if you set goals that are not true for you. So tell the truth before declaring your goals to others.

Be persistent and never give up. Stick with your goals even if you find that they are harder than you thought they would be, or even if you start having doubts about your ability to succeed. Your persistence is important and builds strength inside of you by going beyond where you thought you could go.

Big goals attract big challenges.

Remember that the bigger the goal, the more you will be challenged. You will be tested by these challenges and it will determine your commitment. Use the challenges to get stronger and you will be able to play a larger game.

When you set a big goal, you may come face-to-face with your own fears. Fear is not real; it is imagined and is something that you learned from others. The only way that fear can be transformed is through self-love. Establish a self-love ritual, such as the Emotional Freedom Technique (EFT) or other energy releasing processes to help you walk through your fears or other emotions that may be arising around the goals that you set.

The Purpose of Goals

- Goals direct your focused attention and intention.
- Goals must be written down or they are just ideas.
- Goals are something that you are really interest in and passionate about.
- Goals are something that you are willing to work hard to make happen.
- Goals facilitate momentum being built.
- Goals must be distinct in their purpose; they can be grouped into the important categories of your life such as personal, business, health, well-being, spiritual, emotional, family, friends, marriage, financial, career, etc.
- Goals require daily action.
- Goals are the solution to the problems you are having.

- Goals are the answer when you do not know what to do.
- Goals must be reached for daily!

Desires and Wishes

- Desires and wishes are your daydreams, and are perfectly okay—just don't confuse them with your goals.
- Desires and wishes are things you want, or places you want to go, yet you will probably never take an action or set a goal to achieve.
- Desires and wishes are not goals.

Goals Strategy

- A goals strategy includes where to start, the middle, and the end result.
- A goals strategy has a timeline.
- A goals strategy is the map that guides you in achieving your goals.

Energy of BEE-ing

- BEE-ing is about the part of you that helps you cross the finish line or start a business or purchase a house. Your BEE-ing is the essence of who you are in the world; it is what people know you for and it is what you want to be known for as well.
- BEE-ing produces energy, and that is what people feel when you connect your soul to your goals.
- Taking actions in the energy of BEE-ing produces the results that you desire to achieve.

JAN H. STRINGER *and* ALAN HICKMAN

Here are your guidelines for setting goals in the energy of your BEE-ing:

1. To start, select one goal. Use the criteria listed on the previous pages. Be specific and write it on a piece of paper. Writing your goals down is a very important part of this process.

2. Create a BEE-ing statement in the same way that you created one when working with the BEE-ing Attraction Plan in Part 4. Make it a title if you like and be sure it is something that inspires you and makes you giggle with delight! This is who you will be BEE-ing when you are working on your goal.

3. Next identify the action steps that will accomplish your goal. Write the actions down underneath your goal. Be specific. Give a timeframe in which you accomplish this action.

Below is an example of the setting goal process that Jan used to complete the writing project of this book:

My Goal is: to complete writing my book by March 4th.

My BEE-ing is: I am BEE-ing a channel through which the impossible becomes possible.

My Action Steps:
1. To identify where to add additional stories to each of the chapters by Tuesday
2. To identify the testimonials that I want to use in each chapter by Tuesday
3. To insert the stories and testimonials into the chapters by Wednesday
4. To review each chapter and make revisions by Saturday
5. To write the last two chapters by Sunday

Once you identify your goals, you can add them to your BEE-ing Attraction Plan on Part 3. You will want your BEE-ing Attraction Plan to reflect your goals as a reminder of what is important to you, also to connect your goals to what makes you tick *and* your BEE-ing declarations.

"I set a goal of attracting one hundred participants in my Twitter Smart class within the next seven days. Then I created my BEE-ing as the "Marketing Magician." From that place of BEE-ing, I took the actions required to promote the class, such as set up the event in my web site, establish the date and time, write the copy for the promotion, and then send it out to my list. Within five days eighty people registered for the class." —ALAN

The next part of your action steps involves focus and dedication to keep on keeping on! Be persistent and keep reaching for your dreams and aspirations. You will never know how some of your goals will be manifested; however, what is clear is that consistent action taken towards the fulfillment of your goals, from the place of your created BEE-ing, will produce energy. This energy is what will help you to stay connected to your desires and will fuel your enthusiasm. Your customers will feel this energy of your BEE-ing because it is very attractive. People want to do business with people who are successful and reaching for their goals. Your perfect customers want what you want and feel it when you are making an effort to reach a goal. They want to help you get there.

When you reach 75 percent of your goal, such as Alan did in the example above, it is time to set a new goal! To keep the results happening requires reaching for your goal and it requires a new BEE-ing to have a 100 percent success.

For example, when Alan had set his original goal of one hundred participants in his class within a week, after he had seventy-five registrations it was time to up his goal. Why? It takes a new goal and a new BEE-ing and new actions to reach to the next level.

JAN H. STRINGER *and* ALAN HICKMAN

"After reaching for my goal of one hundred people and having so many registrations, I now set my goal to be two hundred during the next week. I created my BEE-ing as "the Exuberant Unstoppable Marketing Magician." Now this week I will take new actions so that I keep on reaching for my new goal. By setting my goal and BEE-ing, I can see there are some new actions that I have not taken yet that will allow me to reach even farther than before."—ALAN

When you are setting goals that are in alignment with your BEE-ing Attraction Plan, you will be able to determine the best, most attractive action to take. For example, in Alan's example above, just the act of setting a new goal and BEE-ing gave him new ideas and insights that he had not utilized yet in his promotion goal. The act of reaching for your goal sends out an energy that is felt by others who are sensitive to your vibe. Remember, your perfect customers want what you want and will also want you to succeed in reaching your goals.

Actions are *not* your goals!

Are you someone who lives by your to-do list? Many people make elaborate lists of things that they must do and think that these actions are the same as their goals.

For example, Shirley had a goal of connecting with her clients and promoting her services through a monthly newsletter.

Her actions steps involved researching newsletter formats, creating a format for each newsletter, gathering news and items for the first newsletter, writing the newsletter, creating a subscription list of her clients, then ultimately sending it out.

Since Shirley had set the goal of connecting with her clients, she can feel the sense of pride that she had when her first newsletter went out. If she had only focused on checking off her list of to-dos, she would never have reached a goal because there will always be more to-dos. When you feel overwhelmed or unappreciated it is because you have not established goals to focus on and get caught in the endless cycle of your never ending to-do list.

Dazzling distractions or attractive actions?

Additionally, when you are undecided about something or about which direction to go, it is because you are not connected to what makes you tick. When you are not connected to your BEE-ing Attraction Plan and what makes you tick, then you may be dazzled and go off your path. In these times, you may become distracted. Any activity or project that takes you off your path and away from what makes you tick is called a *dazzling distraction*.

Your BEE-ing Attraction Plan together with your Goals Strategy will keep you focused on your game and taking attractive actions that are in alignment to what makes you tick, which is your true purpose in every business activity.

Who are you BEE-ing when you take actions on your goals?

Lastly, when you are rooted and grounded in what makes you tick and you are taking actions from your BEE-ing, you will create what marketers and branding experts call a **buzz**— a term that fits in so well with the analogy of the bumblebee! Your business will thrive like a bee hive does when the bees are working to produce the honey.

"When the bee buzzes onto your path, it's a reminder that with hard work and a firm commitment to building your dreams, a sweet outcome is assured. The bee is a symbol of luck, so expect miracles and your life will be victorious and sweet. Remember that you also create your own luck. That is, effort is essential as you progress along your path in order to make your dreams a reality. The bee is an industrious, busy creature that's always making honey. The bee 'gets busy,' and that honey will soon be yours. The bee is always a fortunate omen." —COLETTE BARON-REID

CUSTOMER STORY

To Have What You Don't Have, You Get to BEE Who You Aren't BEE-ing!

BY ALAN DAVIDSON

"For any outcome you want, there is a certain way of *thinking* and *acting* that will get it for you. You have to find that way of thinking and acting, and then *adopt it*." —BILL HARRIS

The White House called my cell phone today. And so did Tim Geithner's office. He's the US Secretary of the Treasury.

You see, I have a dream. I want to speak at a Democratic National Convention. Now—I have no illusions of running for public office. I have too many skeletons in my closet for that. But this I know...

This spiritual healing that humanity and the world needs right now to solve the myriad problems that plague us must include healing human consciousness and engaging the political process. The crushing pressure of financial fear, desperate poverty, eroding environment, the zeitgeist of war zones, torture, and terror demands a paradigm shift in our thinking, our actions, and our BEE-ing. My speaking at the Democratic National Convention would be a keystone of spiritual intelligence intersecting with political practicality.

Alas, the White House and Tim Geithner's office weren't calling for me—yet!

They were calling for the man sitting next to me, Congressman Barney Frank, *the* Barney Frank, in the last three weeks famously seen on *Meet the Press*, *Face the Nation*, *This Week with George Stephanopoulos*, and *The Daily Show with Jon Stewart*; and now appearing in the back seat of "Ms. Scarlet," Scotty Cole's vibrant red Ford pick-up truck. We were escorting Barney from the airport across town and catching a quick interview on the way. Barney's cell phone was dead, so his Washington office gave my cell phone number to the White House. (Next time they'll be calling for me).

A lot is made about the Law of Attraction these days. It's pretty simple, really: Ask, Attract, and Allow.

- Asking as clearly, powerfully, and descriptively as possible for my heart's desire sets the Universe in motion.
- Attracting is easy—the Universe works intelligently to create, co-create, and manifest our desires for us.
- Allowing is the synchronization with and acceptance of my heart's intention.

It is the allowing that causes the most confusion and disappointment. Why is it, when I ask for something—when I desire it wholeheartedly—that it seems to take forever (or never) to manifest? That is the secret to the art of allowing.

And that's where BEE-ing comes into play. Who I am BEE-ing, right now in this moment—is attracting, vibrating, creating, and manifesting every single thing in my life.

Think about that.

Who you were BEE-ing at every level of your consciousness—body, heart, mind, choice, and spirit—is creating everything around you. So if I want to create something new, I get to BEE somebody new; somebody who is in perfect alignment with my new creation.

Makes sense, doesn't it? But the challenge is to know who to BEE. And just as important is how to shift my BEE-ing into that exact match with what I am most desiring and attracting.

I want live in a world of peace, joy, health, and wealth. To that end, I want to speak at a Democratic National Convention. Who do I have to BEE as a spiritual leader (and non-politician) to land a keynote speech at the most watched political convention in the world?

JAN H. STRINGER *and* ALAN HICKMAN

I have to be so clear, so precise, and so powerful in my BEE-ing and my message for healing and change that the convention will reach out and simply ask me to join them. Am I that man right now? No, not yet. But I am becoming that man. I am systematically, carefully, joyfully shifting my BEE-ing into a man who easily speaks for the kind of healing we need right now. And people are listening.

People like Congressman Frank.

Barney Frank, Chairman of the House Financial Services Committee, one of the most powerful men in Washington DC and in the country right now, is sitting next to me on our way to PBS Channel 8. And the White House is calling *my* cell phone trying to reach him.

We call that a sign of land. Sailors who have been at sea for long periods of time can tell when they're approaching land many miles before they see the shore. First, there might be a bird flying, then twigs or leaves floating in the water, and finally the horizon peaks before they stand firmly on dry land, their voyage complete.

This simple metaphor is an example of the art of allowing. How we see little signs along our way that support our highest intention. The signs show our efforts to change and show us that our shift in BEE-ing is paying off. We haven't quite landed safely yet, but we are well on our way.

So the White House calling my cell phone on a Tuesday afternoon in Houston, Texas is a sign that I am on track; that if I continue to systematically change who I am BEE-ing into a more clear, loving, and powerful teacher—who eloquently and charismatically shares my message of possibility for our world—the White House will be calling me.

Now all that may sound touchy-feely and very nice and sweet, in a Hallmark card kind of way. Shifting my BEE-ing may be simple— but it's not always easy. For me to become the kind of man that is a keynote speaker at a national political convention, I have to dig down deep to my toenails to wrestle with the darkness, and the shadows, and insecurities that live there. I have to be willing to shine the light of truth and love in all the places that I've been afraid to look. I have to shine so brightly that no one can miss the beauty of my message—the beauty of my BEE-ing.

The map that I use for shifting my BEE-ing is what I call mastering my Five Vital Intelligences: my physical, my emotional, my mental, my moral, and my spiritual IQs. This map gives me a way to measure, track, boost, and improve each of my vital intelligences. As I heal my body, heart, mind, choice, and spirit, I become a dazzling attraction. As I hone my skills as a thinker, speaker, and teacher, I attract that keynote speech at the Democratic National Convention. I not only have to heal from the inside, I have to perfect my skills on the outside. This dramatic shift in BEE-ing is not for the faint of heart. It requires diligence, intention, and attention: and most of all it demands courage.

So I'm thrilled the White House called my cell phone and it wasn't for me. I'm thrilled the US Secretary of the Treasury called my cell phone and it wasn't for me. I'm thrilled I was sitting next to Congressman Barney Frank. They are all signs of land. They are the clues that I'm on my right track, that my BEE-ing into the man I most want to BEE in the world is happening. I am evolving, healing, and loving my way into BEE-ing. And I love it!

It is one thing to write a BEE-ing Attraction Plan. It is one thing to desire something. It's one thing to declare to the Universe, "I will be someone who has this, my heart's desire."

It's quite another to quietly, elegantly, and efficiently shift my BEE-ing into the person who is—who gets to BEE—that which I most desire. And that is the real secret to BEE-ing and the art of allowing.

ALAN DAVIDSON, MASTER STRATEGIC ATTRACTION™ COACH, AUTHOR OF *BODY BRILLIANCE*, HOUSTON, TX / WWW.THROUGHYOURBODY.COM

> "For those established in self-referral consciousness,
> the infinite organizing power of the Creator
> becomes the charioteer of all action."
> —RK VEDA, 1.158.6

JAN H. STRINGER *and* ALAN HICKMAN

RESOURCES

Books, Movies, and Teachings

Abraham-Hicks Publications, *Ask and It is Given*, www.abraham-hicks.com

Alan Davidson, *Body Brilliance: Mastering Your Five Vital Intelligences*, www.throughyourbody.com

Bee Movie, www.beemovie.com

Colette Baron-Reid, *Wisdom of Avalon Oracle Cards*, www.colettebaronreid.com

David Deida, *Dear Lover* and *The Way of the Superior Man*, www.deida.info

David McArthur, Bruce McArthur, Linda Brown, *The Intelligent Heart*, www.intuitive connections.net

Debbie Rosas & Carlos Rosas, *The Nia Technique*™ www.nianow.com

Deborah Shames and David Booth, *Speaker Survival Guide*, www.eloqui.biz

Don Miguel Ruiz, *The Four Agreements*, www.miguelruiz.com

Dr. Joe Dispenza, *What the Bleep Do We Know!?* www.whatthebleep.com

John O'Donohue, *Anam Cara: A Book of Celtic Wisdom*, www.johnodonohue.com

Dr. Judith Orloff, *Emotional Freedom, Positive Energy*, www.drjudithorloff.com

Florence Scovel Shinn, *The Game of Life*

Janet Attwood, Chris Attwood, *The Passion Test*, www.thepassiontest.com

Jamie S. Waters, *Big Vision, Small Business*, www.ivysea.com

John Penberthy, *To Bee or Not to Bee*, www.ToBeeBook.com

Lynn A. Robinson, *Trust Your Gut*, www.lynnrobinson.com

Mariaemma Willis, *Discover Your Child's Learning Style*, www.mariaemmawillis.com

Michael E. Gerber, *The E-Myth Revisited*, www.e-myth.com

Nancy Cleary, *A Book is Born*, www.WyMacPublishing.com

Paul and Layne Cutright, *You're Never Upset For the Reason You Think*, www.paulandlayne.com

Richard Bartlett, *Matrix Energetics: The Science and Art of Transformation*, www.matrixenergetics.com

Sonia Choquette, Ph.D., *The Psychic Pathway*, www.trustyourvibes.com

Susie Duke, www.investmentadvisorsinternational.com

The Daily Om, www.dailyom.com

Unity School of Christianity, *Daily Word*, www.dailyword.com

13 Moon Natural Time Calendar, www.13moon.com

Energy Teachers, Energy Medicine, and Personal Healing

Alan Davidson, *Psych-K; Big Mind Meditation*, www.throughyourbody.com

Amazon Herbs, www.lifeismagic.com

Brad Yates, *EFT, Tap O' The Morning*, www.bradyates.net

Byron Katie, *The Work*, www.thework.com

Dr. Barry Morguelan, *Morguelan Energy Institute*, www.energyforsuccess.org

Essential Oils, www.younglivingoils.com

Gary Craig, *Emotional Freedom Technique (EFT) Insights Newsletter*, www.emofree.com

Jin Shin Jitsu, www.healthatyourfingertips.com

Joe Nunziata, *Energy Clearing*, www.jnunziata.com

Judy Morris, *Feng Shui, and Energy Clearing*, www.fsrc.net

Landmark Education, *The Landmark Forum*, www.landmarkeducation.com

Paul and Layne Cutright, *Innovators of Relationship Energy RePatterning*, www.paulandlayne.com

Satyen Raja, *Warrior Sage, Sex, Passion & Enlightenment, Illumination Intensive*, www.warriorsage.com

Shirley Norwood, Psych-K; Hellerwork, *Heart-to-Heart Communication*, www.shirleynorwood.com

Business Consultants, Mentors, Trainers, and Coaches

Adrienne Leigh, MBA, MA, Business and Financial Consultant, www.murphybusiness.com

Brian Tracy, Speaker, Consultant, www.briantracy.com

Carolyn Fine & Associates, Business Consulting, www.carolynfine.com

Daniel Quat, Daniel Quat Photography, www.danielquatphoto.com

David Krueger, MD, Executive, and Mentor Coaching, www.mentorpath.com

Deanna Rutherford, The Rainmaker Extraordinaire, www.rainmakerextraordinaire.biz

Deborah Shames and David Booth, Communications Company, www.eloqui.biz

Doug Upchurch, Insights Learning and Development Company, www.insights.com

Gina Gaudio-Graves, IM University, www.askggg.com

I Learning Global (ILG), The Largest On-line Learning Library, www.ilearningglobal.biz/perfectcustomers.com

Jo Stepanenko, Century 21 Superstars Orange County, www.jostep.com

Lynn A. Robinson, Intuition Teacher, Business Consultant, Intuitive Insights, www.lynnrobinson.com

Marty Marsh, Soul Proprietor Coach, www.soulproprietorcoach.com

Nancy Cleary, Indie Publisher and Custom Publishing Imprints, www.wymacpublishing.com

Paul and Layne Cutright, Relationship Coaching, www.paulandlayne.com

Sonia Choquette, Psychic and Spiritual Teacher, www.soniachoquette.com

Stella Hollett, CEO & Senior Consultant, Insights Atlantic, www.insightsatlantic.com

Susie Duke, Investment Consultant, www.investmentadvisorsinternational.com

Suzy Giraud, Director of Wowieekazawiee Creative Camps, suzg@cox.net

Zoe Jarboe, Psychic and Spiritual Teacher, www.GoddessBizBlog.com

SACAT: Licensed and Certified Strategic Attraction™ Coaches:

Alan Davidson – Houston, TX – Body, Mind, Spirit, www.throughyourbody.com

Annie Sherwood – Houston, TX – Jewel Beams anniesherwood@yahoo.com

Betsy Sobiech – Chicago, IL – Tiara: The Exceptional Women's Coaching Program, www.tiaracoaching.com

Betty Healey – North Lancaster, Ontario, Canada – The Road Signs Coach, www.roadSIGNS.ca

Cheri Valentine – Nashua, NH - Relationship Coaching, www.cherivalentine.com

Don Giberson – Hamilton, Ontario, Canada, Certified Law of Attraction Trainer, www.dreamcrafters.ca

Emily Dabney – Chicago, IL – Personal Co-active® Coach, Certified Nia Technique™ Teacher, emdabney@aol.com

Eva Gregory, CPCC – Emeryville, CA - Master Law of Attraction Coach, www.LeadingEdgeCoaching.com

Frieda Fox – Houston, TX - www.Choose.FreeLife.com

Janet Wise – Hollis Hills, NY - WISE MasterMind Alliance/WISE Power Parties/Wise Connections, www.wisesolutions4u.com

Jennifer (Brugh) Tanguy – Houston, TX – www.jenniferbrugh.com

Julia Stege – Sebastopol, CA – Branding from the Heart, www.graphicgirlz.com

Linda Grace – Aptos, CA – lindabgrace@gmail.com

Margaret Hickman – Bristol, UK – Master Law of Attraction Coach, www.abundancequeenbee.com

Mariaemma Willis, M.A. – Ventura, CA - LearningSuccess™ Programs, www.mariaemmawillis.com

Monique Toh – Indonesia - motoh@wt.net

Nancy Klarman – Keene, NH - protégé@CreativeYankee.com

Pat Altvater – Waterville, OH - Transforming Bodies and Minds, www.womenoutsmartingweight.com

Patty Walters – Houston, TX – Life is Better with a BOA, www.i-shiftnow.com

Rick Stoddard – Phoenix, AZ – rickstoddard@cox.net

Shirley Norwood – Austin, TX – The Heart Listener, www.shirleynorwood.com

Sylva Dvorak, Ph.D. – Pacific Palisades, CA - Consultant, Counselor and Public Speaker, www.atmaninternational.com

Wendy Watkins – Atlanta, GA – People and Business Growers, www.passionfruitpeople.com

For more information:

SACAT: Strategic Attraction™ Coaches Academy and Training, www.perfectcustomers.com/SACAT

or contact: customerservice@perfectcustomers.com

Photograph © 2009 Daniel Quat

JAN H. STRINGER *and* ALAN HICKMAN

ABOUT THE AUTHORS

Jan H. Stringer, founder, PerfectCustomers, Inc., co-author of *Attracting Perfect Customers: The Power of Strategic Synchronicity*, the groundbreaking book that launched their proprietary book and programs in 2000. Jan is a visionary, speaker, coach, facilitator, and business intuitive. She also is founder of Strategic Attraction™ Coaches Academy and Training (SACAT), a licensing, and certification program. SACAT began as a result of their many loyal and dedicated customers requesting to share this work in their own businesses. Additionally, a BEE-ing Attraction Planner Facilitator training program is available as part of the Strategic Attraction Coaches Academy and Training (SACAT).

For more information about becoming a SACAT and training to facilitate the BEE-ing Attraction Planning process effectively for yourself, your clients, or within your company or organizations, go to: www.perfectcustomers.com/facilitator

Alan Hickman, founder, PerfectCustomers, Inc is a transformational catalyst, relationship intuitive and the world's greatest cheerleader. He facilitates programs: BEE-ing Attraction Mini-'BEE' Course, Attracting Your Perfect Mate, and Setting Goals in the Energy of BEE-ing. For more information about upcoming teleclasses, go to www.perfectcustomers.com/events. Alan has authored several e-guides and home study online programs, and reports. For more information, see: www.perfectcustomers.com/reports.

Additionally, he coordinates joint ventures and Internet marketing for the company, as well as their web sites and blogs.

Jan and Alan bring a rich combination of their passion and intimate partnership to business plus their success tool, BEE-ing Attraction, that will benefit every type of business and relationship. Their vision is to work with people to discover deeper connections within themselves to develop, more heart-centered business.

Jan and Alan share their marriage and business from their home in Santa Fe, New Mexico. You can reach them at: jan@perfectcustomers.com or alan@perfectcustomers.com.

For more information, go to
www.perfectcustomers.com *and* www.GoddessBizBlog.com

INDEX

A

Achieving vs. allowing, 184–185
Actions vs. goals, 191–192
Activation of attraction, 3–4. *see also* BEE-ing Attraction Plan
Active listening, 22. *see also* Listening
Acupressure, 102
Advice, 122
Alice's Adventure in Wonderland, 153
Allowing vs. achieving, 184–185
Appreciation, attention and, 100–101
Appreciation Journals, 101
Attention
  appreciation and, 100–101
  attraction and, 56
  of audience, 23
  energy and, 74
  listening and, 22
  signs and, 81
Attitude, 46
Attracting Perfect Customers: The Power of Strategic Synchronicity (Stringer), 1, 22–23, 178, 180
Attraction
  activation of power of, 3–4
  vs. distractions, 192
  energy balance and, 91–92
  explaining, 55–66
  feelings surrounding, 134
  Law of, 26, 30–31, 35–38, 46, 72, 76–77, 100, 105, 106–107, 131, 139–142, 178, 194
  self-check for, 95
  timing and, 107–108
Audiences, speaking to, 21–22
Awareness
  energy balance and, 97–98
  self-. *see* Self-awareness
  signs and, 87–88

B

Balance
  attraction and, 91–92
  exercise for, 92–93
  keys for maintenance of, 95–99
  presence and, 94–95
BEE-ing, identification of, 39–53
BEE-ing Attraction Plan
  during challenges, 47–48
  connection with self and, 145–152
  creation of, 39–53, 157–158
  defined, 2–4
  energy balance and, 98–99
  goal-setting and, 183–196
  instructions for, 164–177
  intention and, 146–147
  marketing and, 8
  paradigm shifts and, 41–42
  partnerships and, 138–139
  passions and, 30–33
  perfect fit and, 153–156
  persistence and, 49–50
  self-awareness and, 42–47
  templates for, 159–163
  writing, 146
Big Vision, Small Business, 133
Body Brilliance, 196
Booth, David, 17
Branding from the Heart, 37
Breathing exercises, 117
Burning bowl ritual, 126–127
Business, heart-centered, 7–13

C

Calendars, 105
Candles, 117, 124
Carroll, Lewis, 153
CEO, embracing title of, 50–53
Certification, 2
Challenges, 47–48, 187–188
Chaos, 76
Childhood, 47–48
Choices, 76

Choquette, Sonia, 67
Clarity, 12
Clearing space, 118–119
Cleary, Nancy, 29–30
Communication, of desires, 71
Community, 12, 115. see also Space
Confidence, speaking from the heart and, 19, 25
Consciousness-building, 3
Corrections, 137
Courage, 11, 12
Creation, of BEE-ing, 39–53
Creativity, 3, 11
Cutright, Layne, 55
Cutright, Paul, 55

D
Dabney, Emily, 63–66
Daily Om, The, 79
Daily Word, The, 94
Davidson, Alan, 193–196
Decision-making, 70
Declarations, for BEE-ing Attraction Plan, 176–177
Desires vs. goals, 188
Discover Your Child's Learning Style, 114
Dispenza, Joe, 45–46, 49
Distractions, 192
Downsizing, business creation and, 10
Dreams, intention and, 134
Dreamweaver's program, 65
Duke, Susie, 180–182

E
E Myth Revisited, The, 40
Economy, changes in, 10
Eloqui, 17, 23
Emotions. see also Space
 attraction and, 59–62
 creating space and, 115
 release of, 117
 signs and, 80, 83
Empowerment, speaking from the heart and, 19
Energy
 attention and, 74
 attraction and, 62–63
 balance of. see Balance
 BEE-ing Attraction Plan and, 3
 creating space and, 117
 goal-setting and, 188
 Law of Natural Time and, 106
 speaking from the heart and, 17
Environment, 15, 115–116, 128–130. see also Space
Essential oils, 103, 117
Exercises, energy balance, 92–93, 97–98
Expectations, clarification of, 171–175

F
Faith, 11, 67
Family, 115–116
Feelings, invocation of, 20–21
Feng Shui, 115
Flowing vs. pushing, 185–186
Focus, 12, 95–97
Four Agreements, The, 121
Future, intention for, 133–142

G
Game of Life, The (Shinn), 87
Gerber, Michael, 40
Giraud, Suzy, 33–34
Goal-setting, 3, 46–47, 183–196
Guidance (inner). see Intuition

H
Healey, Betty, 89–90
Healing, attraction and, 62–63
Heart-centered business, 7–13
Hickman, Alan, 147–150
Hicks, Abraham, 92
Holding space, 119–123
Honesty, 56–57, 186–187

I
Image, speaking from the heart and, 19
Imagination. see Creativity

Improvisation, speaking from the heart and, 24–26
Incense, 117, 124
Inner guidance. *see* Intuition
Intelligent Heart, The (McArthur and McArthur), 7
Intention, 133–142, 146–147
Intuition, 11, 67–78, 186–187

J
Jin Shin Jitsu, 102
Journaling, 101

K
Kitchen table planning, 13–16
Krueger, David, 96

L
Law of Attraction, 26, 30–31, 35–38, 46, 72, 76–77, 100, 105, 106–107, 131, 139–142, 178, 194
Law of Natural Time, 106
Learningsuccess Institute, 114
Letting go, 123
Licensure, 2
Lighthouse test, 108–110
Lighting, 117
Listening, speaking from the heart and, 21–23, 25
Love
  BEE-ing Attraction Plan and, 12
  business/marketing and, 8
  critical nature of, 1
  of self, 25

M
Marketing, 8
McArthur, Bruce, 7
McArthur, David, 7
Meditation, 102, 117
Mental representations, signs and, 80, 83–84
Midlife Crisis Begins in Kindergarten, 114
Money, energy balance and, 101–102

Morguelan, Barry, 91
Morris, Judy, 115

N
Nia Technique, 116, 119
Nutrition, 102

P
Paradigm shifts, 41–42, 108
Partnership, 23–24, 25, 138–139
Passions, identification of, 29–38, 169–170
Past experiences, BEE-ing Attraction Plan and, 47–48
Peace, BEE-ing Attraction Plan and, 11
Pelullo-Willis, Mariaemma, 111–114
Penberthy, John, 39
Perfect customers, identification of, 164–168
Perfect Customers, Inc., 13–16, 27, 35, 99
Perfect fit, identification of, 153–156
Persistence, 49–50, 137–139
Personal issues, attraction and, 59–62
Perspective, honoring of, 24
Physicality, 80, 82, 115, 128–130. *see also* Space
Power of You Now!, 114
Preparation, speaking from the heart and, 26
Presence, 11, 25, 94–95, 117
Projection, 57–59
Purpose, identification of, 29–38
Pushing vs. flowing, 185–186

Q
Quantum physics, 45–46

R
Reflection. *see* Meditation
Relationships, 11, 12, 56–57
Religion. *see* Spirituality
Responsibility, 3, 56
Retreats, 127–128

Robinson, Lynn, 68
Ruiz, Miguel, 121
Rumi, 157

S

SACAT. *see* Strategic Attraction Coaches Academy of Training
Sacred spaces, 123–127
Secret, The, 46, 178
Self, connection with, 145–152
Self-awareness, 18–19, 24–25, 42–47, 62–63, 70
Self-care, 101–103, 129–130
Shames, Deborah, 17
Sharing, 17–19, 26–28, 47. *see also* Speaking
Sherwood, Annie, 150–152
Shinn, Florence Scovel, 87
Signs
   asking for/receiving, 85–86
   awareness of, 87–88
   from emotional realm, 83
   as guideposts, 87
   from mental realm, 83–84
   from physical realm, 82–83
   representations of, 80
   significance of, 79–81
   from spiritual realm, 84–85
   threes and, 81–82
Sobiech, Betsy, 139–142
Space, 115–131
Speaking
   Board of Directors and, 19–20
   from the heart, 17–19, 26–28
   improvisation and, 24–26
   invocation of feelings and, 20–21
   listening and, 21–23
   with partners, 23–24
   visualization and, 21–22
Spirituality, 80, 84–85, 115, 123–127. *see also* Space
Stege, Julia D., 35–38, 100
Strategic Attraction Coaches Academy of Training, 2, 13–16, 27, 65, 84, 85, 111, 114, 138, 140, 150, 152, 170, 178–180

Strategic attraction planning, 1–2. *see also* BEE-ing Attraction Plan
Stringer, Jan, 1, 13–16, 29, 118–120, 147–150

T

Tanguy, Jennifer, 155–156
Teamwork, 25. *see also* Partnership
Templates, for BEE-ing Attraction Plan, 159–163
13 Moon Natural Calendar, 105
Tiara: The Exceptional Women's Coaching Program, 139–142
Tick Words, 35–38
Timing, 105–114, 135–136
To Bee or Not to Bee (Penberthy), 39
Tracy, Brian, 74
Trust, 11, 67–78, 186–187
Truth, 186–187

U

Uncertainty, 185
Understanding, 12
Upchurch, Doug, 50–53

V

Vibrational energy. *see* Energy
Visualization, 21–22, 117, 147. *see also* Intention

W

Walters, Jamie S., 133
Walters, Patty, 13, 24, 26–28
Watkins, Wendy, 178–180
What the Bleep do We Know!? (Dispenza), 45, 49
Wishes vs. goals, 188
Wowiekazowiee Creative Camps, 34
Written notes, 46
Wyatt-MacKenzie, 29–30, 211

Wyatt-MacKenzie Publishing, Inc.
DEADWOOD, OREGON

Can we help you find your perfect publishing option?
Visit www.WyMacPublishing.com.

Breinigsville, PA USA
16 February 2010
232588BV00001B/5/P